Linoleum Block Printing

Linoleum Block Printing

FRANCIS J. KAFKA, Ed. D.

Professor of Education, Millersville State College,
Millersville, Pennsylvania

DOVER PUBLICATIONS, INC., NEW YORK

This Dover edition, first published in 1972, is an
unabridged republication of the work originally published in 1955 by McKnight & McKnight Publishing
Company.

International Standard Book Number: 0-486-20308-5
Library of Congress Catalog Card Number: 72-79299

Manufactured in the United States of America
Dover Publications, Inc.
180 Varick Street
New York, N.Y. 10014

TO

MOTHER AND DAD

Introduction

This book gives the home craftsman and student the basic information required for practicing the art of printing with linoleum blocks. The decoration of fabrics and other materials by block printing can be noted in history as long ago as the time of the early Egyptians and Chinese, in the eras before the high development of decorative arts in Western civilization. It is a fascinating craft and obviously met man's need for reproducing a single repetitive design on his possessions.

Fortunately for the beginner, the materials and equipment needed for linoleum block printing are inexpensive, easily obtained, or easily made or improvised. In no other area of the graphic arts can a rolling pin or a spoon be used as an effective substitute for a printing press. In no other area of the illustrative arts can the amateur craftsman meet with such immediate success as he can in block printing. There is something primitive and pleasantly quaint in those designs most readily adaptable for block printing, giving the beginner a feeling that he does not have to spend a lifetime mastering a complicated series of skills in order to practice the craft.

The entire area of block printing, using linoleum or other simple materials, serves as an excellent introduction to the vast field of illustration in the graphic arts. It is easily observed, through this simple material, how the development of the highly skilled crafts of woodblock engraving, copper or steel engraving, and in present times, photo-mechanical platemaking, took place. Although the home craftsman or the student at school cannot experience the thrill of transforming a photograph or intricate hand-drawn design into a product that can be used to reproduce countless copies of the original, with imagination and through the medium of a linoleum block, he can experience the excitement of seeing his own design printed many times over. He can use it for decorating products of everyday use, such as greeting cards or paper napkins. He can use it to add a personal touch of originality to his letterheads and notepaper. And he can use it in the ever-widening field of hand-decorated fabrics. This latter can be in the form of an original monogram on a shirt, tie, or scarf, or it can be in the form of a repeat design on table cloths or yard goods. The field is practically unlimited.

Some of the material in this book is reprinted because it has withstood the test of time. Much of it is completely new. The book was written to teach linoleum block printing to beginners. It is presented in such a way that the beginner is able to go right to work. After a brief history of the craft, an experimental project is offered for immediate practice. Rather than grouping all the technical information in one section it is scattered throughout the chapters. Thus, almost each project discussed uses a different technique for cutting, a different technique for printing, and frequently a different type of paint. Through this system of progression the craftsman can proceed at his own rate of speed and experience the enjoyment of completing useful objects before he has completely mastered all the technical information presented. Even the lists of materials and equipment have been deleted from later chapters, where it is believed that the beginner no longer requires this repetition.

After the first experimental work the reader is given a very complete analysis of materials and techniques needed for success. This is considered to be of importance because most of us like to know just "what type" and "what kind" is meant. Specialized information is included in a section called *"additional hints"* at the end of various chapters. A *calendar of projects*, listed on page 81, will be of value to the student and the home craftsman. It offers suggestions when the individual's imagination is at low ebb. A carefully chosen *bibliography* is given for those who care to proceed to more advanced and specialized block printing.

All the projects in the book are simple and basic. No previous knowledge or skill is presumed. The instructions are written in step-by-step procedures, with an emphasis on illustrations rather than on words. The book has been designed to help the student and the home craftsman to enjoy many happy hours as they pursue the various phases of this pleasant craft.

Francis J. Kafka

Acknowledgments

The author wishes to express his sense of gratitude to many people and many organizations for their contributions. All have made the task of preparing this book more pleasant and much simpler.

The following industrial manufacturers were especially kind in furnishing photographs and other materials: The American Crayon Co.; *The American Home* Magazine; American Type Founders, Inc.; Armstrong Cork Co.; Behr-Manning Corp.; The Carborundum Co.; The Chandler & Price Co.; The Challenge Machinery Co.; Eastman Kodak Co.; M. Grumbacher, Inc.; C. Howard Hunt Pen Co.; Ideal School Supply Co.; Millers-Falls Co.; The Rosenthal Co.; Southern Skein & Foundry Co.; Vandercook & Sons, Inc.; F. Weber Company; X-Acto Crescent Products Co., Inc.

The Metropolitan Museum of Art, New York City, The Chicago Natural History Museum, and the Scalamandre Museum of Textiles in New York City were all most generous in offering their historical material for my use.

Individuals too numerous to mention have assisted in many ways in both word and deed. I wish to express thanks to Mr. John A. Spelman, III, for his offer to furnish many of his most magnificent block prints; to Mr. S. William Janes of the Elijah D. Clark Junior High School, New York City, for never forgetting to be both friend and teacher; and to Mr. Bernard A. Seckendorf, a young man of unusual and singular talents, not the least of which is the possession of an ever-present helpfulness in many small ways too numerous to count.

For assistance in the always arduous task of proofreading I owe thanks to Mr. Otto Kafka, Mr. Charles William Phillips, and Helen K. Perry.

Table of Contents

CHAPTER I

A History of Block Printing

From the earliest times block printing has served man as the means by which he could reproduce, many times over, the pictures he had drawn. It served man in the same manner in which movable type was to serve him after its invention. Between the two techniques, the field of graphic arts was born. Man was able to print many copies of his written words, many copies of his pictures or drawings, and then bind them together into books. In simple terms, these activities are the graphic arts.

In this book emphasis is placed on one phase of the art of reproducing drawings or pictures from a relief surface. There are many other techniques for accomplishing this purpose; many are used more frequently. However, the basis for the technique is the same no matter what material is used. Metal, wood, and plastic are probably more used commercially; but in each case, a drawing or a design must be created in relief so it can be imprinted an almost unlimited number of times.

The earliest illustrations were hand-applied to individual products. Thus a caveman, to cite the earliest example would draw a picture on the wall of his cave. Later in history he began drawing pictures on his pottery, his baskets, and his clothing. This was the art of illustration in its original form. However, no two illustrations could be alike since each was drawn separately, and directly on the product. This form of illustration persisted throughout the ages, sometimes becoming highly personalized, as in the application of a monogram or an initial; and at other times becoming almost public by its nature, as in the paintings and frescoes in churches and public buildings.

The first method of recording information to pass on from generation to generation was handwriting or copying — those who could write composed huge volumes of material. All illustrations necessary were drawn, also by hand. Most readers are familiar with the beautifully illuminated books copied by hand by monks in the Middle Ages. Here even the capital letters of each paragraph were ornately designed and decorated in color and gold leaf.

Long before the writing of books, however, man was striving to find a method for reproducing pictures so that many could enjoy them. He was also interested in printing a design in a repeated pattern on his clothing and other of his possessions. Thus we find that the ancient Chinese, Assyrians, and Egyptians began experimenting with block printing. Wooden and stone blocks were used, the design being scratched or carved out of the surface. Ink or dye of some type was applied to the surface, and then, by inverting the block an imprint of the design could be made. By repeated inking and imprinting, the design could be reproduced as often as desired. The art soon spread to Japan where wood was used exclusively as the medium and a highly specialized skill resulted. Block prints dating from as early as the 8th and 9th centuries have been found in China and Japan.

While block printing grew in the East, it didn't seem to develop to any great extent in the West, which was meanwhile producing highly complex ornamentation on metals, shell, leather, and glass. Thus the skilled artisans were at hand, ready-made as it were, to turn their hands to a new medium. The earliest woodcut from Europe is dated somewhere in the 15th century. Fig. 1 is an example of an old woodcut of this approximate period. It will be noted from this illustration that the technique used (and also the one used in the Orient) was to remove all the wood from the background leaving just the outline or the "black line" areas to print.

Prior to the invention of movable type, but after the development of woodblock printing, books were made by engraving a block of wood for each page, including wording as well as illustrations. These blocks were then used to print the sheets which were later bound into books. Fig. 2 illustrates this type of woodcut.

With the invention of movable type in Europe the woodcut became the means for inserting illustrations into printed material. (It is

Fig. 1. A Woodcut of the Early 15th Century

WALTER CRANE. *Illustration from The First Book of the Faerie Queene*

153

Fig. 2. A Page Which Is Completely Engraved

interesting that even today, despite the material from which the illustration is made, the printer still refers to it as a "cut.") With the European skill at engraving metals and precious stones, the woodcut soon gave way to engraved plates of steel or copper. These enabled the craftsman to accomplish finer lines and the finished cut also lasted longer than did wood. Woodblock printing almost faded from the scene.

Sometime toward the latter part of the 18th century a revival of the art of woodblock cutting was stimulated in England. It was at this time that the "white line" method was introduced. In this method the background of the block remained intact and printed in a solid color, while the design itself was carefully cut out and showed white on the printed page. At this stage of the craft the cutting of woodblocks could almost be called engraving, so fine were some of the lines.

In the Orient the woodblock seemed to retain something of its original purpose, and was used more and more for the printing of fabrics. To this day in India some fabrics are printed by the ancient method of carving a design from a large block of wood, applying dye to it, and stamping it onto the cloth. Fig. 3 shows one such woodblock from India, and Fig. 4 illustrates a native Indian craftsman working at a piece of cloth. In the background can be seen samples of other woodblocks which he uses.

Until comparatively recent times the engraved copper plate or steel plate was the main method of illustrating books. Lithography, or the process of drawing on specially-treated stones with special paints, and then pressing the sheets to be printed against these stones, was a development when printing in more than one color was demanded.

With the development of the modern printing press, methods of making reproduction cuts by photographic and chemical means were invented. These processes are of a highly technical nature and volumes have been written on each. In the chemical method metal is deposited over the surface of a printing block by electroplating. This thin shell of metal is removed, reinforced with base metal, and used as a print-

Fig. 3. A Woodblock Used in India Today (Courtesy of the Chicago Natural History Museum)

Fig. 4. An Indian Cotton Printer at Work (Courtesy of the Chicago Natural History Museum)

ing plate. Additional printing plates can be made from the original. In the photographic method, a picture is printed on a metal plate with a sensitized surface. In the developing of the printed picture, acid is allowed to dissolve the portions of the plate not wanted while the design or picture remains intact and forms the printing surface. Recently plastics, that all-embracing medium, has entered the field of plate- or cut-making and printing cuts are now made from it. Fig. 5 illustrates several commercially-made cuts. Note that the metal or plastic cut is mounted on a block of wood. In many large industrial printing plants, especially for newspaper and periodical publishing, the cuts are made of solid metal. In general, however, even in the most modern of printing establishments, the craftsman returns to the 7th or 8th century and mounts his printing plate on a wooden block.

Woodblock engraving remains today as something of an art unto itself. Except for fine, privately printed books made especially for collectors, and possibly selected greeting cards and book plates, most illustrations today are printed from photo-mechanical-chemical plates. These are usually referred to as "half-tone" cuts, because of a special process resembling cross-hatching, which enables the plate-maker to produce halftones or mixtures of whites and blacks (gray).

Some twenty-five years ago, after linoleum had become the popular floor covering that it still is, craftsmen discovered that it had many

Fig. 5. Some Modern Commercially-Made Cuts

qualities which made it an ideal medium for cutting in the manner of the older and more difficult-to-cut woodblock. This immediately opened new horizons for the amateur craftsman. Linoleum was cheap, of even, smooth texture, fairly easy to cut or engrave, tough

Fig. 6. A Modern Book Illustration Printed from a Linoleum Block

enough to withstand the pressure of printing, and produced a handsome print almost identical to the woodblock print. Many artists and craftsmen turned toward this new medium, and the ancient art or block printing has returned with renewed vigor and some remarkable results. A few books in modern years have been entirely illustrated with linoleum block prints. Fig. 6 shows one taken from such a book*. Numerous greeting cards are printed with linoleum blocks. And so popular have block-printed fabrics become that most of these are printed on rotary printing presses to imitate hand-blocked prints!

* John A. Spelman, III, *At Home In the Hills.* Pine Mountain, Kentucky: Pine Mountain Print Shop, 1939. Reprinted with permission of the author.

CHAPTER II

Experimenting With the Simple Block Print

The beginner in block printing will do well to try a simple method of accomplishing a print before going on to the more difficult techniques. The budding craftsman will want to cut a design into some material which is easy to cut. This will produce the printing block. He will want a simple method of placing ink on his design, and finally, a simple method of transferring this ink on to a paper surface.

It is not necessary to go far to find simple materials with which to experiment. A small, hard potato, a block of gum eraser, a discarded bottle cork, or a length of half-inch dowel stick; each of these may be used for simple block-print making.

Fig. 7. Some Simple Materials Used in Block Printing

Materials and Equipment

Small, hard potato, *or*
Block of gum eraser, *or*
Bottle cork, *or*
Dowel stick, 6 x ½ inches
Small artist's paint brush
Water color paint in several colors
Sharp pocket knife
Colored construction paper
Ruler
Pencil
Wiping cloth (waste rag)
Small dish of water
Artist's oil paints
Spirits of turpentine

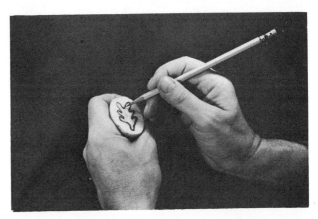
Fig. 8. Drawing a Design on a Potato

Procedure

1. Cut the potato in half.

2. Wipe the moisture off one cut surface and with a pencil draw a small design on this surface, Fig. 8.

3. Using the pocket knife, carefully go over the pencil lines, cutting into the surface of the potato to a depth of about one-quarter inch, Fig. 9. Then cut so that the background can be lifted out, leaving the design standing out in relief on the surface of the potato, Fig. 10. Lift out all of the background, leaving a raised surface

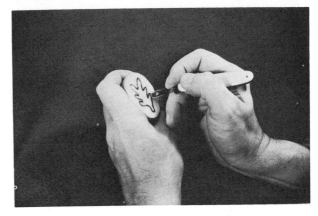
Fig. 9. Cutting Around the Design

of the original design, similar to a piece of type. From this it is possible to print many copies of the design.

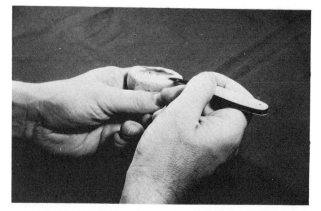

Fig. 10. Cutting Away the Background

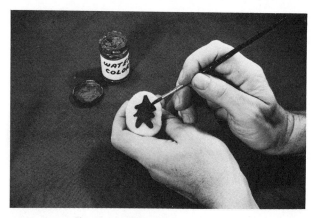

Fig. 11. Applying Paint to the Design

Fig. 12. Printing the Design on Paper

Fig. 13. Repeating the Design

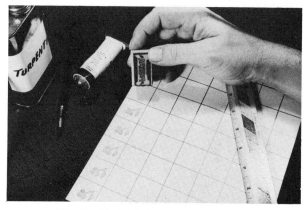

Fig. 14. Block Printing with a Gum Eraser

4. With a small artist's brush apply a thin coating of water color paint to the entire surface of the design, Fig. 11.

5. Hold the potato block as you would a rubber stamp, and print the design onto a piece of construction paper. Be sure that the paper is of a lighter color than the color of the paint being used, Fig. 12.

6. Using the ruler and pencil lay out a sheet of the construction paper in squares or rectangles, with each dimension about $\frac{1}{4}$ inch larger than the size of the design. An interesting repeat pattern can be produced by block printing the design in each of the boxes, Fig. 13. The block will have to be re-inked with water color paint for each impression. After a number of impressions have been made, dried paint will tend to build up on the surface of the design. This can be removed by dipping a corner of the wiping cloth into clear water and washing the surface, being careful not to damage the potato. Construction paper, so printed, makes an attractive book jacket.

7. Because of the water content of the potato, only water-soluble paints can be used for this type of simple block printing.

8. For a higher degree of permanency, as well as for printing on washable fabrics,

an oil-soluble paint should be used. Oil paint cannot be used on the watery surface of the potato so the design must be cut into the surface of a gum eraser. The same procedure is used for making the block and printing it, except that turpentine is used for cleaning, rather than water, Fig. 14.

9. A bottle cork or a length of dowel stick may be used as the block for variations in size and design. The texture of the cork will usually show through the paint, creating an interesting appearance. The dowel stick is very convenient for small designs to be used as repeats around the border of an object. Oil paints are used on these blocks, as the cork and wood will both absorb too much of the water from water paint, Fig. 15.

10. A cork or eraser block can be inked by pressing it on a rubber stamp pad as shown in Fig. 16. However, the quantity of ink which is taken from the stamp pad is slight, and the imprint can be made successfully only on light-colored paper with a hard finish.

Commercially-made rubber stamps such as those shown in Fig. 17 are very similar to the somewhat crude block which has been cut from a potato or a gum eraser. In the rubber stamp the letters or designs are molded in rubber so that they stand up in relief. Ink is applied by pressing the stamp on an ink pad. The stamp in turn is impressed upon a sheet of paper. It will be noted in all relief printing that the original design is reversed.

Study the techniques of transferring the design to the block, cutting the block, inking the block, and transferring the design to paper or cloth in any desired arrangement before going on to more advanced stages of block printing.

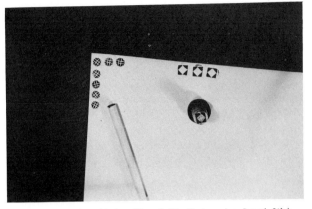
Fig. 15. Designs Made with a Bottle Cork and a Dowel Stick

Fig. 16. Using a Stamp Pad for Printing

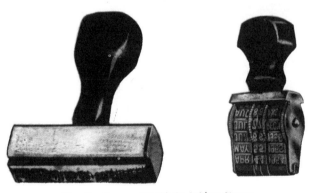
Fig. 17. Commercially-Made Rubber Stamps

CHAPTER III

Introduction to Linoleum Block Printing

In the early days of block printing, as noted in Chapter I, the craftsman had to spend many years developing the skill required to do intricate engraving on the face of blocks of wood. Even when the designs were simple, the craftsman was working with a material which was hard to handle and which allowed for no errors. Later, metal plates instead of wood blocks were used but here again the craftsman had a difficult material with which to work.

Although the illustrations for many fine books and greeting cards are made from woodcuts or steel and copper engravings, most of this hand work has given way to the chemical and photo-mechanical methods of making printing plates. But the craftsman who is looking for a simple inexpensive material with which to work, yet one which produces nearly the same results as a woodblock cut or a copper engraving will find linoleum nearly ideal. Linoleum has long been used as a floor covering because of its qualities of semi-softness and long life. In addition, it is waterproof and has a very fine texture, which very closely resembles fine, end-grain wood. Its elastic quality means that it has a certain "give" which makes it wear well, even under great pressure, when used as a printing block. Designs are easily cut into its surface.

The tools, materials, and equipment needed for linoleum block printing are simple and inexpensive. Many of them can be made at home or in the school shop. The following list is basic. Additional special items will be mentioned under subsequent chapter headings. Following this listing, each item is discussed more fully to help develop a sound understanding of the tools and materials of the craft. The items listed under *Materials* are those which normally are consumed in use or wear out in use. Therefore these have to be continually replenished in the school or home shop. Those items called, *Tools and Equipment* need be purchased just once, since with care they last a lifetime.

Materials
Battleship linoleum
Draftsman's tracing paper
Typewriter or pencil carbon paper
Thumb tacks
Gummed cellulose tape
Graph paper
Water color paint
Oil colors
Printer's ink
Spirits of turpentine
Kerosene
Eraser
Drawing ink
Sandpaper
Glue
Paper for printing
Cloth for printing
Waste rags
Pencil

Tools and Equipment
Ruler
Pocket knife
Sharpening stone
Mallet
Spatula
Brayer
Drawing pens
Bench hook
Artist's brush
Glass
Linoleum block cutting tools
Printing press

Battleship Linoleum
This variety is made in $\frac{1}{8}$-inch and $\frac{1}{4}$-inch thicknesses. It is a solid color, usually tan or white, and is backed with burlap, Fig. 18. Linoleum especially prepared for block cutting is available and is already glued to $\frac{3}{4}$-inch plywood stock, Fig. 19. The surface is colored either white or light grey to make it easier to transfer the design to the linoleum. It is not necessary, however, to purchase these ready-made blocks. Chapter IV describes how battle-

ship linoleum is glued to a wooden block. Fig. 20 illustrates an assortment of sizes of commercially obtainable linoleum blocks which are sold by the square inch.

Draftsman's Tracing Paper

This is a high quality of tissue-type paper which has a dull finish, will take pencil marks and is very transparent. As a substitute, the "second sheet" or "onion skin" paper used for making carbon copies of typewritten letters may be used. This latter is not as transparent nor as tough as tracing paper, however, and will rip more easily.

Typewriter or Pencil Carbon Paper

Typewriter carbon paper is the ordinary type used for making duplicate copies on the typewriter. Pencil carbon paper is softer and will make a darker line. Both are manufactured by mixing lamp black with waxes and oils, and coating a layer of this mixture onto a thin, tough paper. This layer of black wax is transferred onto another sheet whenever an impression is made on the back of it. Carbon paper should not be confused in name with tracing paper.

Thumb Tacks

Any good variety will do the job of holding designs and other pieces of paper in place. However, the variety known as "drawing pins" have an extra large head and are easier to pull out and replace.

Gummed Cellulose Tape

The transparent variety or the opaque variety are both satisfactory for this work. These tapes are superior to the gummed tape which has to be moistened with water because they stick to any type of surface and can be more easily removed.

Graph Paper

One-quarter inch ruled or that commonly known as four-to-the-inch, is the best for this work. Graph paper is used for enlarging and reducing designs, which is explained in Chapter VII, and to make it easier for the amateur craftsman to draw his own designs.

Water Color Paint

Actually this name can be applied to any paint which dissolves in water. For linoleum

Fig. 18. A Piece of Battleship Linoleum

Fig. 19. Ready-Prepared Linoleum Mounted on a Plywood Block
(Courtesy of M. Grumbacher, Inc.)

Fig. 20. An Assortment of Commercially-Obtainable Linoleum Blocks

block printing, however, it is necessary to have an ink that will adhere evenly to the somewhat oily surface of the linoleum and still dissolve in water. There are several very fine, water-soluble block printing inks available commercially. These have the advantage of keeping well in tube form and of having a heavy body which can be reduced with water as desired by the craftsman, Fig. 21. If ordinary water paint is used, the variety called "show card color" or "tempera," which is obtainable al-

Fig. 21. Reducing Water-Soluble Paint

ready mixed in jars, is the type that should be used. To this is added a little glycerine to make it adhere to the linoleum.

Oil Colors

As the name implies, these colors are soluble in some form of oil rather than water. Turpentine and linseed oil are usually the liquids into which the colors are mixed. Ordinary artist's tube colors can be used, thinned down with a small quantity of spirits of turpentine. This type of paint must be used carefully if printing is being done on soft papers. The paper very often draws the oils from the paint, forming a large greasy area around the printed design.

Printer's Ink

This is the ink used for commercial printing. It is available in a large variety of colors and can be purchased in small quantities in tubes. It is probably the best all-around ink for the block printer, as it can be used on paper as well as on cloth. It is, however, oil-soluble, which means it cannot be washed free with water.

There are basically two types of paints used in this craft. One is water-soluble, the other oil-soluble. Obviously the water-soluble is neater and cleaner. However, the craftsman must decide on the ultimate use of what he is printing. If the article will receive wear and moisture, then the oil-soluble ink will have to be used. If it is to receive actual wetting, as in laundering, even the oil-soluble inks will have to have added to them a *mordant* which will make them color-fast. This will be explained in Chapter XII. For the average dec-

orative use, water-soluble paints are satisfactory.

Spirits of Turpentine

The highly-refined type, available in small bottles in art supply houses, is the type preferred. It is a little more costly but of a better quality than the crude variety used for mixing with house paints. Turpentine will serve as a solvent for most types of oil paints.

Kerosene

This is a handy, inexpensive, and safe cleaning agent for equipment, linoleum blocks, and the hands. It burns but it does not explode as benzene may, although the latter is also an excellent cleaner.

Eraser

A soft, clean eraser is best for correcting errors made in pencil drawings.

Drawing Ink

The jet black, waterproof type is needed. This is available commercially in small bottles.

Sandpaper

This should be of a very fine grit, such as 6/0 or 8/0. It is used both to give a keen cutting edge to the linoleum-cutting tools and for removing wax and other unwanted surface materials from the linoleum.

Glue

Any good brand of ready-mixed, animal or vegetable glue may be used for attaching the linoleum to a wooden backing block.

Paper

A fairly heavy, dull-finish paper is best because it absorbs the ink more readily and gives a more attractive finish. For ordinary work colored construction paper is excellent. For finer work, the craftsman may want to try Japanese handmade paper, though it is considerably more expensive. Bookpaper of about fifty to sixty pound substance, known as "antique" and "eggshell," is a fine all-around paper for use in the school shop.

Cloth

Block printing may be accomplished on almost any type of cloth fabric, but a finely woven cotton or linen material is easiest. Silks require the utmost of skill because of their flimsiness, and the synthetic fabrics do not always take the ordinary paints and dyes too well. Wool is satisfactory if the weave is fairly fine and tight.

Waste Rags

These are for cleaning; they must be free of buttons, clips, snap fasteners, and other items which might damage the surface of the linoleum.

Ruler

A steel one is preferred, although a wooden or plastic one is quite satisfactory. It is important that it have a neat, straight edge.

Pocket Knife

It should have at least two blades of different sizes, both extremely sharp.

Sharpening Stone

Actually two are required, Fig. 22. One is used for sharpening the knife and the flat portions of the outer edges of the cutting tools. The honing slip is especially designed for sharpening the inside of "V" and round cutting tools or gouges. A little water or machine oil should always be used on a sharpening stone to prevent excessive wear and to help carry off the ground particles of metal.

Mallet

Either a wooden, rawhide, or plastic mallet may be used to strike the back of the mounted linoleum block and make a more satisfactory impression, Fig. 23.

Spatula

This is sometimes called an ink knife. The thin, flexible steel blade is used to measure out and mix paints, Fig. 23.

Brayer

This is also called an ink roller. The solid rubber or gelatin roller, or a rubber-covered wooden roller, is fitted into a convenient holder with a handle. It is used to spread ink and paint into a very thin film and to apply this ink or paint to the block which is to be printed, Fig. 23. Some experiments have been made with a piece of rubber hose fitted into a handle made from a wire coat hanger, but such devices are not very satisfactory. A good brayer is not very expensive and even this cost

Fig. 22. Sharpening Stones (Courtesy of Behr-Manning Corporation)

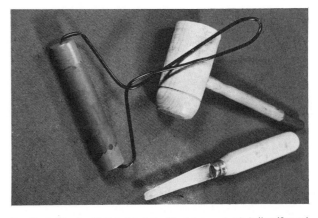

Fig. 23. A Wooden Mallet, Ink Knife (Spatula), and Ink Roller (Brayer)

can be minimized by purchasing a small photographic print roller.

Pencil

A soft drawing pencil is preferred, as its markings can be easily erased. It should be kept well pointed, sharpening it in a machine or with a knife, and then using sandpaper to put a final finish to the point.

Drawing Pens

The drawing pen with the reservoir type tip is recommended. These pens come in an assortment of shapes as well as sizes. It is suggested that one shape be chosen, preferably the round, and that all five or six sizes within this shape be purchased. One penholder will be sufficient, as the pens are interchangeable. Fig. 24.

Bench Hook

This item will be found in any well-equipped craft shop, or it can be made in a half-hour

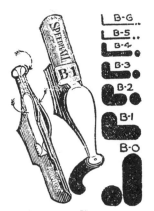

Fig. 24. Drawing Pens and the Different-Sized Marks they Make
(Courtesy of the C. Howard Hunt Pen Co.)

Fig. 27. A Bench Hook in One of the Possible Positions

Fig. 25. A Bench Hook

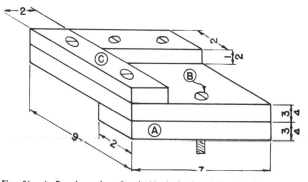

Fig. 26. A Drawing of a Bench Hook Designed for Linoleum Block Cutting

by any craftsman. It is simply a device which fits over the edge of a workbench or a table, or can be fastened into a woodworker's vise, enabling the craftsman to do small work which might otherwise mar the surface of the table. Because of its construction it also helps make those cuts when the working piece has to be kept from slipping but cannot be fastened down. Fig. 25 shows the bench hook attached

to a table top, while Fig. 26 is a working drawing of a bench hook designed for linoleum block cutting.

The bench hook has a movable lower piece, A, Fig. 26, which holds it against the bench edge. Normally this piece is fastened down in the same manner as the top piece. In this design this lower piece is pivoted at B on the drawing with a $\frac{1}{4}$-inch bolt fitted with a wing nut, enabling the operator to swing the surface of the bench hook to any convenient angle. In addition to this modification, the bench hook has a left edge stop, C on the drawing, as well as a back stop so that the linoleum can be held against the left side as well as against the back. These two stops are fastened down with flat head wood screws, countersunk. Fig. 27 illustrates the bench hook in one of the possible positions. As will be emphasized later in the book, the bench hook is also a safety device which prevents the craftsman from running the cutting tool into his hand.

Artist's Brush

This will be used for applying drawing ink to large areas before cutting the design and in some cases, for applying paint or ink to the surface of the block to be printed. A number four camel's hair or red sable, round, is an ideal size for general use.

Glass

A sheet of glass of the type known as "plate glass," about 12 x 12 inches is ideal. It is used as a slab for mixing inks and paints with the brayer. Glass is most practical because it is non-porous and can be cleaned very easily. Be sure to have the glazier from whom the glass is purchased file down the sharp edges.

Linoleum Block Cutting Tools

These are especially made or commercially manufactured for this use alone. There are several commercially-made sets on the market which have many advantages. They are not expensive. A very practical set is shown in Fig. 28. In this type the actual cutting tool is no larger than a drawing pen and each size and type of cutter fits into one handle. The price is low enough for the student or home craftsman to replace them as they dull. The handle will last almost indefinitely. Another type of cutter is shown in Fig. 29. In this type the cut is made by "scooping" out the unwanted material instead of gouging it out as in the conventional method of carving. Still another type is shown in Fig. 30. This type, far more expensive, is very similar to a small-sized wood-carving tool. These cutters are made of high grade steel, can be sharpened and honed as any high quality cutting instrument can, and represent a permanent investment.

The student or home craftsman may like to try his hand at making his own set of cutting tools from discarded umbrella ribs. These are made of a fairly high quality steel and can be hardened, tempered, and sharpened.

Procedure for Making Cutting Tools

1. Obtain a supply of each of the two sizes of umbrella ribs which are found on a discarded umbrella. Make sure that the ribs are of steel.
2. Cut the ribs into three- or four-inch lengths. This can be done with a hack saw or a file. If the file is used, just nick the rib with a file and then break it by hand.
3. With a pair of pliers, squeeze the rib together at one end. Force this end into a wood file handle, Fig. 31. If the file handle does not have a hole in it, drill one slightly smaller in diameter than the end of the umbrella rib. Drive the rib into the handle about one inch.
4. Heat the other end of the umbrella rib in the flame of a kitchen gas stove, or with an alcohol torch, until it is bright red, Fig.

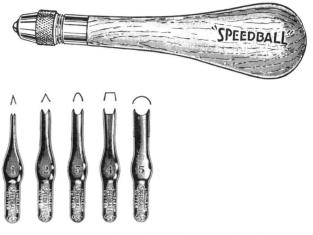

Fig. 28. A Set of Linoleum Block Cutting Tools (Courtesy of the C. Howard Hunt Pen Co.)

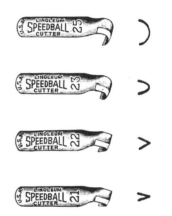

Fig. 29. A "Scooping" Type Set of Linoleum Block Cutting Tools (Courtesy of C. Howard Hunt Pen Co.)

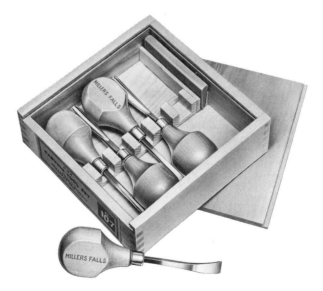

Fig. 30. A More Expensive Set of Linoleum Block Cutting Tools (Courtesy of the Millers Falls Co.)

Fig. 31. Making Your Own Cutting Tools

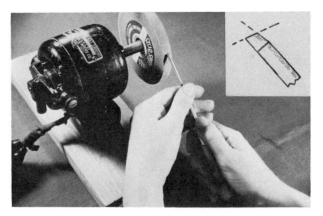

Fig. 34. Grinding the End of the Umbrella Rib

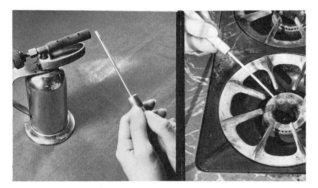

Fig. 32. Heating the Umbrella Rib

Fig. 35. Wearing Safety Glasses While Grinding

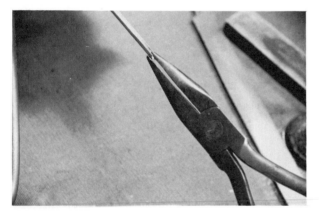

Fig. 33. Shaping the End of the Umbrella Rib

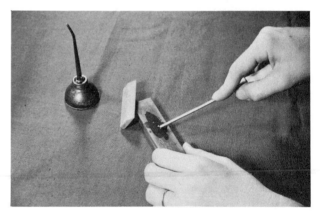

Fig. 36. Sharpening the Tool

32. While the rib is still hot, shape the end into any of the shapes desired, Fig. 33.

5. When the end is shaped, heat it again until it is bright red. Then quickly plunge it into a glass of cold water to harden the steel.

6. Grind the end of the umbrella rib so that it has an angle of slightly less than ninety degrees across the tip (see the insert in Fig. 34). Then put a beveled edge on the rib, Fig. 34. Note in Fig. 35 that safety goggles are being worn to protect the eyes from pieces of steel or stone which may fly off the grinding wheel.

7. Finish sharpening the beveled edge on the flat surface of a sharpening stone. Sharpen inside of the edge with the special slip stone, Fig. 36.

Printing Press

This is an optional item of equipment. There are many presses designed primarily for the printing of linoleum blocks. Figs. 37 and 38 show two of these varieties. The press shown in Fig. 38 can be constructed in the school or home workshop. Cut the eccentric-shaped handle with a coping saw from a solid piece of ¾-inch plywood. The press illustrated in Fig. 39 may be purchased from the manufacturer or constructed by the more advanced woodworker. The base, uprights, and cross beam are made from a hardwood such as maple. The uprights are anchored into the base piece with dovetail joints to keep them from sliding out under pressure. The cross beam is attached to the uprights with mortise and tenon joints

Fig. 39. A More Elaborate Type of Press
(Courtesy of the F. Weber Co., Inc.)

Fig. 37. A Commercially-Made Linoleum Block Printing Press
(Courtesy of the C. Howard Hunt Pen Co.)

Fig. 40. A Copy Press

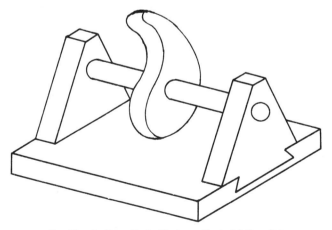

Fig. 38. A Home-Made Linoleum Block Printing Press

to give it adequate strength for the downward pressure. The press board, which is raised and lowered by means of the screw, is made from a piece of ¾-inch plywood. The screw, the threaded plate for attaching to the underside of the cross beam through which the screw passes, and the socket to attach to the press board, are all available from hardware supply houses. These, too, can be made in the machine shop. The screw handle may be turned on the lathe from a piece of maple stock or a discarded table leg may be utilized.

In the school shop a copy press may be available, Fig. 40. This makes an excellent linoleum block printing press. If the proof press,

Fig. 41. A Proof Press (Courtesy of Vandercook & Sons, Inc.)

Fig. 42. Items Which Can Be Used in Place of a Printing Press

Fig. 41, is used, the linoleum must be attached to a block of wood or at least placed over a block of wood, to bring it up to the height of printers' type. It is then inked and run through the press in the usual manner.

The printing press was said to be optional because the items shown in Fig. 42 will be used as much, if not more, than a press in printing linoleum blocks. These items are a rolling pin, a large tablespoon, and a mallet.

CHAPTER IV

The Manufacture, the Use, and the Treatment of Linoleum

The word "linoleum" is derived from two Latin roots: *linum,* which means flax, and *oleum,* which means oil. The flax plant provides linen fibers and its seeds are processed into linseed oil. The two Latin words give the clue that linoleum is made from linseed oil — the same heavy, dark, amber-colored oil that is used in mixing paints.

In 1863 an Englishman, Frederick Walton noticed what the painter notices every time he forgets to cover his can of paint. He experimented with the thick, rubbery skin which formed over the surface of the paint and concluded that the action of oxygen on the linseed oil was the cause of this skin formation. At that time in England many floors were covered with a substance made from rubber mixed with powdered cork. Walton was quick to discover that a fine floor covering could be made by mixing powdered cork with the oxidized linseed oil. A material called *oilcloth,* which was made by placing heavy coatings of oil paint over woven hemp, or burlap was a popular fabric of the time. From this Walton conceived the idea of spreading this newly formed material over burlap, and thus linoleum was born.

As a floor covering, linoleum has the advantage of being resilient and still durable. It insulates from the cold and dampness; and it can be oiled, waxed, or washed. The original technique of manufacturing linoleum was known as the "scrim" method. In this method boiled linseed oil was merely poured over lengths of muslin in a continuous fine stream and permitted to air dry over periods of many weeks. The resulting material, shown in Fig. 43, was cut into chunks, ground up, cured, and then mixed with cork flour. In the modern method the linseed oil is placed in agitating tanks and fine streams of oxygen are forced through the oil. In a comparatively short time the oil absorbs enough of the oxygen to stiffen it into a viscous mass. It is then cured and mixed with resins and cork flour as before. At the same time that cork flour is added, the coloring pigment is introduced. The entire mass is mixed for a long period of time to make sure it is evenly blended. Then the mixture is pressed onto the burlap backing by forcing it and the burlap through a set of parallel rollers similar to those on a wash wringer. The rollers are adjusted to make the linoleum the exact thickness required.

The linoleum is too soft for use at this stage, so it is placed on rollers and baked in special ovens until it is just the correct hardness, Fig. 44.

When a simple substitute for wood and metal plates was sought, linoleum proved to be the perfect answer. The characteristics of linoleum as a floor covering were the same character-

Fig. 43. A Piece of Raw Linoleum Manufactured by an Early Method (Courtesy of the Armstrong Cork Co.)

Fig. 44. Baking the Linoleum (Courtesy of the Armstrong Cork Co.)

istics the craftsman desired. The material had a fine texture, it was resilient, it did not crack easily, and it did not dry out or wear out quickly. Oil as well as water could be applied to its surface without damaging it. In addition to this, the burlap backing made it capable of standing rough treatment, or even being glued to wood without further processing.

The type of linoleum best suited to the craft of block cutting and printing is the type known as battleship linoleum. It is made as outlined above, in a solid or over-all color. Patterned linoleum, though made by a slightly different process, would be satisfactory, except that the pattern and numerous colors make it a confusing medium with which to work. Battleship linoleum, white or tan in color, is available in $\frac{1}{8}$-inch and $\frac{1}{4}$-inch thicknesses. Either color or either thickness is usable, although the white has certain advantages when it is to be drawn upon in pencil, and the heavier weight has the natural advantage of withstanding harder usage.

Fig. 45 illustrates several pieces of both white and tan battleship linoleum. It is sold by the square yard in any floor covering establishment, or it can be purchased in smaller quantities, usually by the square foot, from arts and crafts suppliers.

The first step in preparing linoleum for use in block cutting is to remove the wax protective coating which is usually found on the surface. Wipe the surface very vigorously with a cloth soaked in kerosene. Any of the other excellent wax solvents; such as benzene, lacquer thinner, or naphtha may be used, but with the caution required of all combustible materials. If a very heavy wax coating is found on the linoleum, remove it by scrubbing the surface with fine pumice stone mixed in water, and then wiping with kerosene. Some craftsmen have found it economical to use pieces of battleship linoleum removed from floors. If such material is used it may be discovered that the linoleum has been given a protective coating of shellac or clear lacquer to make it easier to keep polished. If this is the case, experiment until the proper solvent for dissolving this coating is found, and then proceed as outlined.

Rarely will a piece of linoleum be exactly the size required for the project. Therefore it becomes necessary to trim it to the required size. To accomplish this a steel rule or a steel square and a sharp carpenter's knife are all that are required. Guide lines are first made in pencil on the surface of the linoleum. Then, using the steel rule or square as a guide and the knife as the cutting tool, "score" the lines about $\frac{1}{32}$ of an inch into the surface of the linoleum, Fig. 46. Now, with the linoleum over

Fig. 45. Specimens of White and Tan Battleship Linoleum

Fig. 46. Cutting the Linoleum

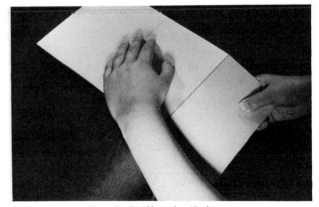
Fig. 47. Breaking the Linoleum

Fig. 48. Cutting Through the Burlap

Fig. 49. A Paper Cutting Machine
(Courtesy of The Chandler & Price Co.)

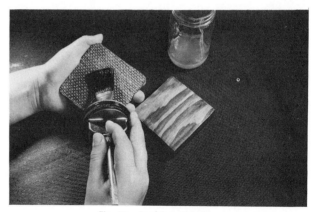

Fig. 50. Applying the Glue

the edge of a table or work bench, press down evenly on both sides of the scored line, Fig. 47. This will crack the linoleum on the line, straight down to the burlap back. Fold it over so that both burlap sides are touching, face in, and cut through the burlap, on a line with the cut in the linoleum, Fig. 48.

If large sheets or large quantities of linoleum are to be cut to similar size, the cutting can be done in the paper cutting machine shown in Fig. 49. When using this machine several thicknesses of heavy cardboard should be placed on top of the uppermost sheet of linoleum so that the blade makes a keen slice through this uppermost piece. Regardless of the method used in cutting, all linoleum should be cut perfectly square. It is for this reason that the steel square is recommended. Perfectly straight, square cuts will eliminate errors resulting in additional work in later steps.

Since linoleum which is fairly warm is more easily cut with the linoleum block cutters the workroom should be moderate, rather than cold in temperature. The piece being worked upon may be warmed on a radiator top or in an oven for a few minutes out of each half-hour that it is being cut. This will keep it in a reasonable state of softness for easier handling.

Often it will be found necessary to mount the linoleum on a block of wood to give it additional support when printing it by hand, and almost always when it is locked up in a printing press. This type of printing will be described more fully later.

To mount the linoleum, cut a piece of wood of about ¾-inch thickness to the same size as the piece of linoleum. Plywood is preferred because it does not warp. The mounting may be done before or after the design has been cut in the linoleum. However, many craftsmen prefer doing it *after*, since the design may be spoiled in cutting and have to be discarded. Spread a thin layer of animal glue on one surface of the block of wood and on the burlap side of the linoleum, Fig. 50. Allow the glue to set for about three minutes and then place the two glue-covered surfaces together. Squeeze the two pieces tightly together by hand pressure, and

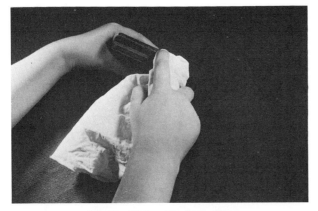

Fig. 51. Wiping Off Excess Glue

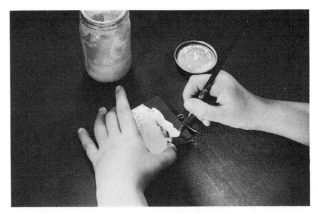

Fig. 53. Painting the Linoleum

Fig. 52. Drying the Glue Under Pressure

with a damp cloth, wipe off the excess glue which runs out along the edge, Fig. 51. Then place a sheet of wax paper on an old board. On top of this place the wood surface of the glued pieces. On top of the linoleum surface place another sheet of wax paper, and a sheet of smooth cardboard. The wax paper prevents accidental gluing together of any of the parts described. The smooth cardboard will prevent the working surface of the linoleum from being marred. Place a reasonably heavy weight on top of the cardboard. A laundry iron or a large book will do. Allow the glue to dry under this pressure for twenty-four hours, Fig. 52.

When working with dark-colored linoleum, it is sometimes advisable (depending upon the method used for obtaining the design) to coat the surface with a light-colored pigment. White tempera paint is best. Stir it thoroughly to mix all of the pigment. Then with a small artist's brush cover the entire surface of the linoleum with an even coating of paint, Fig. 53. Allow it to dry bone-hard (about two hours) before using. Figs. 19 and 20, page 19 show linoleum blocks, commercially available, which have already been mounted on wood and which have a light-colored coating applied.

CHAPTER V

A Basic Project — the Monogram

Tools and Equipment
Soft lead pencil
Ruler
Drawing pens and holders
Linoleum cutters
Bench hook
Mallet
Plate glass
Ink roller
Ink knife, or spatula

Supplies
Graph paper
Carbon paper
Tracing paper
Black drawing ink
Printing ink
Retarding varnish
Glue
Linoleum, battleship, approximately 2 x 3 inches
Woodblock, same size as linoleum
Solid color necktie

A good basic project for the student or home craftsman is a monogram which can be printed on neckties, scarves, and other articles. It is small, compact, and does not require too much planning or cutting. Fig. 54 shows finished items printed according to the instructions given in this chapter.

The first step in planning is blocking out several areas on the graph paper, each 2 x 3 inches. Sketch several shapes and varieties or initials or monograms in these boxes, as shown in Fig. 55. The lightly ruled lines of graph paper make it easier to draw accurate lines freehand. After experimenting with the designs, choose the one which appears to be the best for the purpose and trace it onto a piece of draftsman's tracing paper, Fig. 56. Note that the original drawing and the tracing paper are held securely with gummed cellulose tape to prevent any slipping while the tracing operation is being performed.

Fig. 54. Monogrammed Articles Printed from Linoleum Blocks

Fig. 55. Sketching Various Monograms (Courtesy of Bernard Seckendorf)

Fig. 56. Tracing the Monogram on Tracing Paper (Courtesy of Bernard Seckendorf)

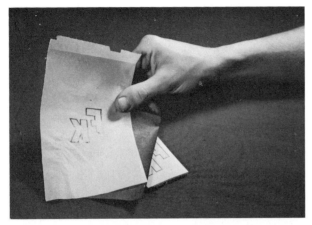

Fig. 57.   Transferring the Design to the Linoleum
(Courtesy of Bernard Seckendorf)

Fig. 58.   Inking in the Design (Courtesy of Bernard Seckendorf)

Fig. 59.   Making the First Cut Around the Outline
(Courtesy of Bernard Seckendorf)

Cut a piece of linoleum about one-half inch larger in each dimension than the size of the monogram to be made. Clean the surface of the linoleum with a little kerosene on a piece of

cloth, then with soap and warm water. Allow it to dry. Place a piece of typewriter carbon paper under the tracing paper in such a way that the carbon is against the underside of the tracing paper. Trace over the complete design, thus transferring the design, *in reverse,* to the back of the tracing paper. This reversed design will be the one used for the finished job. Now place the carbon paper with the carbon side against the smooth surface of the linoleum. Place the tracing paper on the carbon paper so that the *reversed* design is up. Pressing firmly with the pencil, trace over the entire design once again, transferring the design clearly to the surface of the linoleum, Fig. 57.

With a drawing pen and black drawing ink, go over the entire design in outline, following the carbon-transferred lines. Then with a larger pen or an artist's brush and the same ink, completely fill in all of the areas which are to remain intact on the block, as shown in Fig. 58. In this particular project, it is best to make what is known as a positive print. Only the design motif will be printed. Everything else on the linoleum block will be cut away, leaving the design standing in relief, higher than the other surfaces. To avoid making incorrect cuts, completely ink in all areas not to be cut, as instructed above. This is a basic rule which should always be followed.

Place the piece of linoleum on the bench hook for safety in cutting. With the smallest V - shape cutter make a thin cut around the entire outline of the initials as shown in Fig. 59. Note that the piece of linoleum is held against the back stop of the bench hook to prevent it from sliding, and that the hand which is not used to hold the cutter is kept in a safe position *behind* the cutting edge.

Fig. 28 illustrates the sizes of cutters used for this project and all future projects. Using whichever ones are found most convenient for accomplishing the particular cut to be made. Always make a thin, shallow cut in the linoleum, around the design first. The small "V" tool works very well, and for this reason it is usually referred to as the "liner." After accomplishing this first cut around the edge of the design, take the larger V-shaped gouge and make a deeper cut directly over the fine cut made in the previous step, being careful not to cut into the inked area. The inked-in area will not be cut if the *depth* of the cut is guided so that it extends into the un-inked portion of the linoleum. This skill will be rapidly developed with a little practice.

Remove all the linoleum surface which is not part of the design, cutting deep enough toward the burlap backing so that just the design stands out in relief, ready to be inked. The U-shaped gouge is used to make these long cuts from the edge of the design *outward* toward the edge of the piece of linoleum. These cuts are made close to each other so that no high areas or ridges remain. The finished block, as shown in Fig. 60, will have just the inked-in portions remaining.

CAUTION: When cutting around the edge of the design, the cuts should *not* be made perpendicular to the surface of the linoleum, but should slope gradually outward from the outline of the design, as illustrated in Fig. 61, thus giving strength to the portions which remain higher.

If not already mounted, the piece of linoleum should now be fastened to a block of wood as shown in Fig. 62. (See Chapter IV.)

Before printing the block remove all of the drawing ink with soap and warm water. Stubborn spots may be removed with a little rubbing alcohol.

To prepare the ink, mix a very small amount (about the size of a pea) of printing ink of the color desired (remember that light colors do *not* print well over dark-colored materials) and add to it one drop of retarding varnish. If preferred, one of the commercially-prepared hand-blocking inks may be used, mixed according to the manufacturer's directions. Roll the ink out into a thin film on the plate glass, using the brayer or rubber roller, as shown in Fig. 63. Place the article to be printed on a board or a sturdy table top. If it is a large article it should be fastened down with thumb tacks or pins. A necktie, however, can usually be held smooth or will lie flat. It should be unfolded, though, so that the printing is done on *one* thickness of material only.

Run the brayer across the ink several times and then carefully run it across the surface of the design several times, or until the deposit of ink is even, Fig. 64. With a piece of

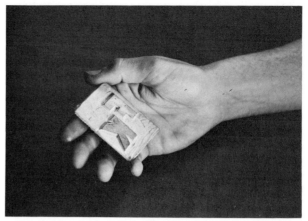

Fig. 60. The Finished Block (Courtesy of Bernard Seckendorf)

Fig. 61. Right and Wrong Ways of Cutting (Courtesy of the C. Howard Hunt Pen Co.)

Fig. 62. The Materials for Printing (Courtesy of Bernard Seckendorf)

clean cloth wrapped around the tip of the finger, carefully wipe away any excess ink which may have been picked up on areas other than the design. Then carefully place the block, inked surface down, against the article to be printed. Be sure it is placed precisely, as it cannot be moved without damaging the print once it has touched the cloth.

Strike the wooden block several sharp blows in the center, being sure to hold the block steady between blows of the mallet (Fig. 65). When the design has been printed onto the

Fig. 63. Spreading the Ink (Courtesy of Bernard Seckendorf)

Fig. 64. Inking the Block (Courtesy of Bernard Seckendorf)

Fig. 65. Printing the Design (Courtesy of Bernard Seckendorf)

Fig. 66. Removing the Block (Courtesy of Bernard Seckendorf)

Fig. 67. "Registering" the Position of the Design
(Courtesy of Bernard Seckendorf)

cloth, lift the block *and* the cloth, and with great care peel the cloth away from the block as shown in Fig. 66. The print should be allowed to air dry until completely hard (at least twenty-four hours) and then be pressed with a hot iron through a clean cloth dampened with vinegar. The print will then withstand dry cleaning or mild hand laundering.

Additional Hints

1. If there is any doubt as to whether the background portions are cut deeply enough, try several prints on a piece of clean, well-pressed cloth. Always remember that once the inked block is struck, wherever a deposit of ink falls, there it remains. It cannot be removed effectively.
2. If the print is to be made on an article where the exact location of the design is of prime importance (such as on handkerchiefs or napkins), it must be "registered." This is accomplished by placing the block, *before* it is inked, on the spot where it is to be printed. Then with strips of gummed tape, mark the outline of the block as shown in Fig. 67. After the block has been inked it can then be replaced for printing.

CHAPTER VI

Block Printing on Paper Napkins or Towels

Tools and Equipment
Soft lead pencil
Drawing pen and holder
Linoleum cutters
Bench hook
Plate glass
Ink brayer
Rolling pin

Supplies
Carbon paper
Tracing paper
Black drawing ink
Printing ink or oil paint
Glue
Linoleum in size required for design
Wood block, same size as linoleum
White or light-colored paper napkins
White or light-colored paper guest towels

Fig. 68. A Simple Floral Design

Fig. 69. A Positive Type Imprint

In this project additional thought is given to choosing the design and to some new technical terms which will make later work simpler. The project — decorated paper napkins or guest towels — is inexpensive and has the mark of individuality.

The design chosen for this project should not be too large. Only a small portion of the paper napkin or towel is visible when folded. It is not considered wise, therefore, to have a design which will fill a larger area than this exposed portion. The design must be appropriate to the purpose for which it shall be employed. It may be drawn to harmonize with other features in the decoration of the room or the home; and may match, or be complementary to, other colors. As the beginner advances in the craft these aspects will become more and more evident. When they are fully understood, a great deal of time is saved by immediately accomplishing the design desired and proceeding with the cutting and printing of it.

A simple floral design, such as in Fig. 68, has heavy lines, is pleasing to the eye, will match well in almost any decorative scheme, and is the type of design which will look well

printed in any color. In this example the printing will be done in one color on a white or light-colored napkin or towel. In the previous chapter the term *positive imprint* was used. This will also be a positive type block.

In linoleum block printing there are three basic types of imprint: the positive, the negative, and the line. Many variations are possible by combining these types. In the positive type imprint, shown in Fig. 69, the design itself is printed while the background portion of the linoleum has been cut away. In the negative

Fig. 70. A Negative Type Imprint

Fig. 72. Preparing the Napkin for Printing

Fig. 71. A Line Type Imprint

Fig. 73. Preparing the Ink

imprint, the reverse is true. The design itself has been cut away and the entire background is printed, Fig. 70. In the line imprint the lines of the design are cut in a fine line technique on a solid background, Fig. 71. It is similar to the negative except that a negative arrangement would require that heavier areas be cut away, while a positive arrangement would be quite difficult and would not print as well. In future chapters all these techniques will be explained and practiced.

Trace the design onto tracing paper and then proceed as in Chapter V, up to and including mounting the linoleum on a block of wood.

Prepare the paper napkins or paper towels for printing by placing a sheet of newspaper under each surface to be printed, Fig. 72. The napkins or towels need not be unfolded for the printing operation if this interleaving with newspaper is done, as the newspaper will absorb any surplus ink which may soak through the thin paper. If it is preferred to unfold them the printing of each piece should be accomplished on a fresh sheet of newspaper. If there is no absorbent sheet beneath the thin paper, the ink will have a tendency to bleed out from the design into the soft fibers of the paper.

Printer's ink, or an oil type of block ink must be used for printing this project because the article is likely to become wet in use. While the article will not be washed, laundered, or re-used, it is not advisable to use any ink which may smear or dissolve while in use. Roll the ink onto the glass plate with the brayer until it is quite tacky, as shown in Fig. 73. This is a basic rule whenever printing is done on thin stock. Spread an even coat of ink onto the linoleum block as described in the previous chapter. Experience has shown that it is not advisable to do much planning for exact register of design in precisely the same location on each article when working with this project. Since the objects are of a disposable nature, the time spent in exact registration is not practical. Of course, the design should appear as close as possible to the same approximate location on each one.

While printing the napkins, the craftsman may wish to experiment with the rolling pin as a printing device.

Procedure

1. When the linoleum block has been inked, allow it to remain in this inked-side up position.
2. Place the area of the article to be printed directly over the inked surface of the linoleum and carefully drop it into place, Fig. 74.
3. Roll the rolling pin, firmly, once across the portion of the paper article which is resting over the linoleum bock, Fig. 75.
4. Peel the article away from the block, Fig. 76.
5. Re-ink the block. Follow the same procedure for each print desired.

Additional Hints

1. Inks of dark colors print well over almost any light-colored paper. Therefore, if a dark-colored ink is used a wider choice of

Fig. 74. Placing the Napkin on the Printing Block

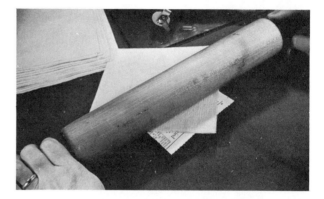

Fig. 75. Using a Rolling Pin to Do the Printing

Fig. 76. Removing the Napkin from the Block

colored paper will be available to the craftsman.

2. The paper towels used in the illustrations in this chapter were made from white crepe paper, cut to required size (approximately 12 x 20 inches) and folded so that the grain of the paper ran the length of the towel. The edges of some were hand cut with scissors, while others were cut with dressmaker's pinking shears.

CHAPTER VII

Greeting Cards

Tools and Equipment
Soft lead pencil
Drawing pens in holders
Linoleum cutters
Bench hook
Plate glass
Ink brayer
Large spoon
Ruler
Basin for water

Supplies
Carbon paper
Tracing paper
Graph paper, four-to-the-inch
Black drawing ink
Water-soluble block printing ink
Glue
Mucilage or paste
Linoleum in size required
Woodblock, same size as linoleum
Colored construction paper
Envelopes for cards
Blotting paper or a blotter book
Brown wrapping paper

The greeting card, regardless of the holiday, offers the greatest opportunity for the craftsman to exhibit his handwork. Nothing is appreciated more by the recipient than a sincere message on an attractive holiday greeting card. When it is the product of the sender himself the significance is doubled.

Fig. 77. A Simple Christmas Card Design

Choosing a design for a greeting card sometimes puzzles the beginner. It has already been suggested that designs be simple and that they emphasize the medium with which the craftsman is working. A greeting card suitable for use at the Christmas holiday is shown in Fig. 77. This type of design in bold silhouette is always appropriate for linoleum block printing. The design may be original or copied from one of many books of patterns. Often, a combination of these methods provides an unusual, yet highly personal, card.

It is often necessary to enlarge or reduce the design to the size required, which is frequently determined by the size of the envelopes to be used. Card envelopes, commonly known as Baronial size envelopes, are available in a large series of sizes, but the following are most often stocked by retailers.

No. 4 Baronial............$3\frac{5}{8}''$ x $4\frac{11}{16}''$
No. 5 Baronial............$4\frac{1}{8}''$ x $5\frac{1}{8}''$
No. 5½ Baronial............$4\frac{1}{2}''$ x $5\frac{5}{8}''$
No. 6 Baronial............$5''$ x $6''$

The card should be made about one-quarter inch smaller than the envelope in both dimensions; and if a margin is required around the design, the linoleum block should be an additional one-quarter inch smaller. Thus, if it is decided to use a No. 6 Baronial envelope, the card will be $4\frac{3}{4}$ x $5\frac{3}{4}$ inches in size. If a margin is required on the card the linoleum block will be, $4\frac{1}{2}$ x $5\frac{1}{2}$ inches in size.

A simple method of enlarging or reducing is the "squaring method."

Procedure for Enlarging or Reducing
1. Draw ruled lines in pencil directly across the design, horizontally and vertically, dividing the design into uniform squares, Fig. 78.
2. If the design is to be enlarged, draw on another sheet of paper the same *number of squares* as on the original design, but make the squares *larger*. The increase in size should be a *proportionate* increase, i.e., 1½ times larger, 2 times larger, 3 times

larger, etc., Fig. 79. When *reducing* the size, the squares are made proportionally smaller.

3. Number the horizontal lines on the original design, starting with number one on the top and continuing down to the last line which crosses the design. Do the same on the vertical lines, starting with number one on the first line at the left of the design. Number the lines on the *enlarged* or *reduced* squares to correspond with the numbers on the original design, Fig. 80.

4. To enlarge or reduce the design, draw one square of the design at a time, carefully noting where each line of the design crosses a numbered line on the original. Fig. 81 shows the original design squared and the enlarged design drawn in.

5. Graph paper may be used if the original design is first drawn or traced onto one-quarter inch graph paper. The corresponding enlargement will then be made two squares larger, or three squares larger, and so on. If a reduction is required, draw pencil lines over the original lines of the graph paper making a new series of squares twice as large or three times as large, and so forth. Using this for the *original* drawing, make the new design on a sheet of graph paper, using the available lines.

For this greeting card a negative imprint will be used. Remember that this technique means cutting the entire design out of the linoleum so that a solid-colored background is printed with the design in reverse, or the color of the paper. This technique is particularly attractive when used on a greeting card, or on any object where the entire surface is to be covered with the imprint, except, perhaps for a narrow margin.

Trace the design *in reverse* (because the wording must be cut on the block in reverse) onto the linoleum. When inking in the design remember that a negative imprint is desired. Therefore, the design will be left free of ink to indicate that this portion is to be cut away. The outside margins of the piece of linoleum in a negative imprint become the border of

Fig. 78. Squaring the Original Design

Fig. 79. Preparing the Proportionally Bigger Squares

Fig. 80. The Numbered Squares

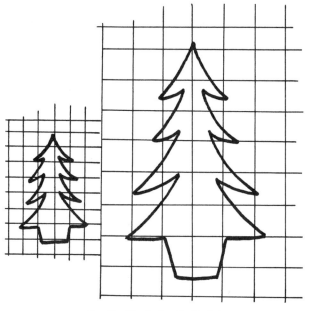

Fig. 81. The Design Duplicated

Fig. 82. A Water-Soluble Ink (Courtesy of M. Grumbacher, Inc.)

Fig. 83. Cutting the Paper (Courtesy of the Ideal School Supply Co.)

the design. Extreme care should be used in cutting the piece of linoleum to assure that these margins are straight and square. See Figs. 46, 47, and 48, pages 28 and 29. After the linoleum is completely cut, mount it on a block of wood.

Water-soluble inks, which are very opaque, look extremely well on a greeting card printed

Fig. 84. A Book of Blotting Paper (Courtesy, Eastern Photo Supply Co.)

on colored construction paper, Fig. 82. Cut the paper to the desired size with scissors, a sharp knife, or by using the card cutter found in many shops, Fig. 83. If a double fold card is desired, the paper will have to be cut *twice* the original width, but the same height. If a four fold, or French fold, card is desired, both dimensions must be *doubled*. The paper used for imprinting with water soluble inks should be especially treated to assure an even imprint.

Procedure for Moistening Paper

1. Obtain a stack of eight or ten large pieces of blotting paper, by cutting several desk blotters into quarters, or purchase them from a photographic supply house, Fig. 84.
2. Soak the cut pieces of construction paper in water for one-half minute.
3. Remove the paper from the water and place them between pieces of the blotting paper. Stack and allow to dry for one hour under the pressure of a heavy book.
4. This stack of blotters, or the blotter book, is known to professional artists as a "damp book." It serves the purpose of thoroughly dampening the fibers of the paper before they are imprinted with the ink.

Procedure for Printing

This negative or reverse print requires an even coating of ink on a large area, so the craftsman is introduced to the "spoon method" of printing.

1. Place the card to be printed on top of the inked surface of the block as in Fig. 74 in the previous chapter.

2. Grasping the spoon so as to use the bottom of it as a rubbing or burnishing surface, rub it evenly and firmly over the entire surface of the card, Fig. 85.

3. Peel the card away from the block and place it aside to dry for at least one hour.

4. Re-ink the block and proceed as before for each card to be printed.

5. Water-soluble ink has a tendency to build up and fill the cut-away portions of the design. If this occurs, clean the block whenever necessary by immersing it in a basin of warm water and then drying it thoroughly.

Procedure for Making Envelope Pattern

Mention was made earlier in the chapter that the card should be made of a size to fit a standard Baronial envelope. However, the reverse of this technique may also be used and an envelope made to fit the size card desired.

1. Secure a sheet of brown wrapping paper twice as large as each dimension of the card the envelope is to be made to fit.

2. In the center of this paper, draw a rectangle which is one-quarter inch larger in each dimension than the card.

3. Using the pattern shown in Fig. 86 as a guide to the shape of the flaps on the completely open envelope, construct the outlines of the flaps. Keep these rules in mind:

   A. Flaps *A* and *C* are first folded inward and fastened with paste at points *x* and *y*. Therefore, one must be a trifle longer than the other so that there will be an overlap.

   B. Flap *D* is then folded up and attached to the lower edges of flaps *A* and *C*. The entire edge of flap *D* must overlap the lower margins of flaps *A* and *C*.

   C. Flap *B* is the one which normally has the adhesive on it and which is brought down and sealed. This flap must be made larger than the others so that it, too, will make the final, required overlapping.

      A little experimentation, with a discarded envelope nearby while the draw-

Fig. 85. Using the "Spoon Method"

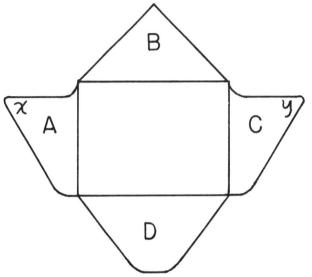

Fig. 86. A Design for Constructing Your Own Envelopes

ing is made, will produce the desired size and shape.

4. Cut the pattern with scissors and trace it onto a piece of sturdy cardboard. This is also carefully cut with strong shears and it becomes the pattern from which each envelope is copied. Any paper may be used for making the envelopes; however, an envelope of matching paper and color compliments the maker of the card to a higher degree.

5. For a school shop, or where the pattern is to be used for hundreds of envelopes, it is suggested that it be made from sheet galvanized iron or sheet aluminum, it will withstand abuse better than the cardboard.

6. For those who may want to apply a moistening type adhesive to the envelopes as well, the following formula is offered.

Dissolve one part of gum arabic in one-half cup of water. Add one part of laundry starch and four parts of granulated sugar. Stir thoroughly to dissolve all lumps. Heat over a low flame until the mixture is completely dissolved and transparent in appearance. Add enough water to make the mixture about the thickness of syrup. A drop of oil of wintergreen may be added to give it a better flavor.

Apply this adhesive to the edge of the envelope flap with a small artist's brush.

Allow it to dry thoroughly before stacking the envelopes or folding down the flaps. At any later date the envelopes may be sealed by moistening the adhesive in the usual manner.

Additional Hints

1. Printing in one color on colored paper results in a two-color pattern.
2. Some light-colored *water-soluble* block-printing inks, recommended for use in this project, *do* print to a certain degree of satisfaction over a darker-colored paper because they are opaque.

CHAPTER VIII

A Letterhead Design Used as a Corner Cut

Whether personal letterheads or noteheads are purchased commercially or printed in the school shop or on a letterpress in the basement home shop, their beauty can be enhanced by the addition of an individualized linoleum block design, Fig. 87. If the printing is to be done by the craftsman or ordered especially for him, it is suggested that it be placed off-center on the sheet in the direction of the right-hand margin, as shown in the illustration. This will allow the design block to fit nicely with the total appearance of the sheet. However, if the printing is already done and it is desired to add a block printed design, it can still be fitted into the layout of the sheet by printing it either to the left or to the right of the name and address lines.

An appropriate design should be picked, one which will add the note of individuality to the letterhead. Flowers and pet animals are frequently the choice of girls and women. Athletic designs and outdoor scenes are favorites of boys and men. The design will have to be small to *enhance* the letterhead or notehead, rather than *dominate* it. Therefore, it will also have to be a simple design to eliminate fine detailed cutting.

For this project the craftsman is advised to use the fine line technique, described in Chapter VI and shown in Fig. 71. In this technique the entire background of the design, the full size of the block, is imprinted, while the design, in fine outline, remains white on the finished project. Of course, if the imprint is made on colored paper, then the design will be the color of that paper rather than white.

Cut a piece of linoleum to the exact size of the corner cut desired, following the steps shown in Figs. 46, 47, and 48, pages 28 and 29. It will not be necessary, for the procedure given in this chapter, to mount the linoleum on wood. The piece of linoleum will have to be perfectly square, however, and have a neat, straight edge all around, as this edge becomes the printed border of the block.

Trace the design onto tracing paper and then proceed as in Chapter V, up to, but not including mounting on wood.

Mix the desired color of printer's ink on the glass plate with the spatula and roll the ink out to a fine layer with the brayer. The color may be either the same as the printing or it may be a shade of this color or a color complementary to it. See Chapter XIII for the suggestions for mixing of colors.

The proof press, shown in Fig. 41, is suggested for the block printing for this project. However, the spoon method or the rolling pin method, explained in previous chapters, may be used.

Procedure

1. Assuming that the letterheads or noteheads are approximately 6 x 9 inches in size, and assuming that the printing of the name and address has been done, or will be done across one of the six-inch edges, obtain a piece of ¾-inch wood, perfectly flat (plywood is suggested), 7 x 10 inches in size.

2. Place this piece of wood on the bed of the proof press. This will serve to bring the printing surface of the linoleum block *up to* the height of type, for which the press is designed. If additional height is required, successive sheets of paper may be placed *under the piece of wood.*

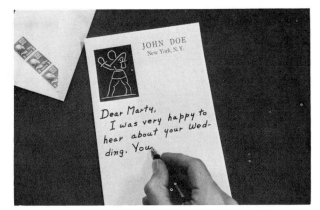

Fig. 87. A Letterhead Design

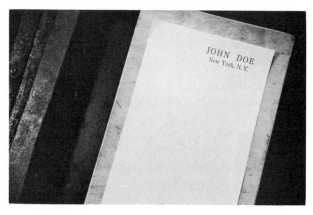

Fig. 88. The Letterhead Placed on the Wooden Block

Fig. 89. The X Marks the Top of the Linoleum Block

3. Place one copy of the notehead or letterhead, printed side facing up, on top of the piece of wood, Fig. 88.

4. Apply a coating of ink to the linoleum block with the brayer.

5. Carefully lift the linoleum block with the hand and place it *face down* on the notehead in the exact location where it is desired that it print. Remember which is the top of the design. An *X* marked in pencil on the burlap backing to designate the top of the design will assist the operator, Fig. 89.

6. Run the proof press *once* across the linoleum block.

7. Peel the sheet away from the linoleum. Repeat the process for each sheet.

8. If a proof press is not available, the rolling pin method or the spoon method of printing may be used, as indicated previously. Since the size of this linoleum block is small, even when these methods are used it is not necessary to mount the block on wood for printing.

Additional Hints

1. Do not operate the proof press more than once for each imprint. If the imprint is too light, additional printings over the same area will not darken it.

2. If the imprint is not dark enough add additional sheets of paper under the wood on the bed of the press.

3. Be cautious of imprints which are so intense that they press into the paper. This is an indication that the printing surface is too *high*, which will damage the linoleum. Remove the paper from under the wood and check the wood to determine that it is the correct thickness.

4. Imprints which appear dark in spots and light in spots are usually the result of uneven inking or a warped piece of wood. Since the proof press applies *even*, steady, and accurate pressure throughout, these defects can be corrected by replacing the wood or by placing additional torn pieces of paper under the wood in those areas which print too light. This is known as "makeready" in the printing industry. Of course if a hand method of printing is used, additional or less pressure applied in various areas will either cause or correct this defect.

CHAPTER IX

Converting a Photograph to a Block Print

A linoleum block print has great possibilities for individual expression when it can be made from a favorite photograph. Converting a photograph into a drawing suitable for linoleum block printing is a knotty problem, though greatly simplified when analyzed, and when a step-by-step procedure is planned. Many beginners have avoided attempting this technique on the assumption that too much skill in art is required. This is not necessarily the case.

The method outlined in this chapter is both simple and effective. In addition, it utilizes home or school photographic equipment and the knowledge that goes with the use of such equipment. The materials and equipment are simple, inexpensive, and easily procured, if they are not already owned. The technique is well within the reach of the beginner. As a matter of fact, anyone who can use a drawing pen and ink to trace simple lines can experiment with this technique.

It is most important to have a good picture. Do not attempt to use any and all photographs merely because the technique is a relatively simple one. It is important in all of the graphic arts to develop the ability to recognize certain photographs as lending themselves more readily to etching, others to engraving, and some to block printing. As pointed out in previous chapters, the block print usually has a feel of solidity about it. The areas for the most part are solid and as large as possible.

The photograph to be converted into a linoleum block print should have the following characteristics:

1. It should be a print of *high contrast*. To those unfamiliar with this photographic term, it means simply that there should be a sharp contrast between absolute blacks and absolute whites on the photograph, Fig. 90. A picture which has an over-all appearance of grayishness is said to have low contrast.

2. It should contain large masses of white and black areas. Country scenes with snow are excellent. Flimsy scenes with delicate and intricate foliage patterns and tree branches are not too easily adapted. Portraits and pictures containing figures of people and animals are not at all suitable for the beginner. Remember that the lines of the photograph will eventually have to be cut out of linoleum. It is possible, as explained later, to remove certain unwanted areas from the photograph, but too much of this removing will not result in a very true duplicate of the original.

3. The photographic print should not have a glossy, waxed finish, but should be what the trade calls, "matte" finish.

4. If a picture is to be taken especially for the purpose of making a block print, it will be more adaptable if orthochromatic film is used. It is also less expensive. The picture will tend to have a higher contrast when taken on this type of film.

For extreme simplicity and as an interesting starting project a picture can be taken with the sunlight shining into the lens, with the camera set at a small lens opening. The resulting picture will be somewhat of a silhouette, making the conversion into a linoleum block even simpler. However, this is not a true type of photograph for conversion, therefore the craftsman may want to omit this experiment.

Fig. 90. A *High Contrast* Photograph (Courtesy of the Eastman Kodak Co.)

Fig. 91. An Inked-Over Photograph

Fig. 93. Cross-Hatching in the Gray Areas

Fig. 92. Ways of Creating Gray Areas

Whether the processing of the film is to be accomplished by the craftsman or by a commercial finishing house, it is suggested that the film be slightly over-developed. This will add further to the high contrast, and since the original tones will be bleached out later on, this over-development will do no harm.

When the picture has been chosen on the basis of contrast, mass, and interest, it remains only to determine the size needed or required. The picture must be of the same size as the finished linoleum block. This may necessitate enlarging or reducing the photograph or cropping it slightly. Experience has shown that

in linoleum block cutting the smaller the block the less detail there should be in the picture, and vice versa. A good, standard size is 4 x 5 inches.

Procedure

1. Study the picture carefully to determine the parts that are specifically white, the parts that are specifically black, and the parts which can be called shaded, or gray.
2. Using waterproof drawing ink and a variety of sizes of drawing pens, ink the areas which were chosen as specifically black areas. These are the areas which will print in the solid color on the finished block. The ink will not adhere well to a glossy print. If the print is glossy and feels as if it has a hard coating, soak it in cold water for about ten minutes, then dry it thoroughly.

   During this step of inking in the solid black areas, a little modification in the original photograph may be necessary. A tree which has numerous fine branches may have to be converted into a tree with fewer and thicker limbs. A building with delicate, latticed windows may have to be converted into a building with heavier lines in the window. Completely unwanted areas such as the figure of a person or an animal can be totally inked over, Fig. 91.
3. A system of dotting and cross-hatching is used by engravers, Fig. 92, to create half-tones, or gray areas. Using this technique,

ink in the areas which are to be shaded in the final print. *Remember that the best block print is one which is of high contrast;* therefore, keep the shaded or halftone areas to a minimum, Fig. 93.

This is the most difficult step in the process and for practical purposes the basic instructions are changed somewhat at this point. Because it is easier when cutting linoleum to do the cross-hatching and shading technique in the manner of a negative imprint (that is, with the actual shading cuts removed against the solid background of linoleum) this is precisely what is done. The objects which are to be shaded (note the bushes in the foreground of Fig. 93) are outlined with ink. The shading marks (cross-hatching, etc.) are also marked with ink. However, when the actual cutting is being done, the entire area within the outline is left intact and the shading cuts are removed. This is actually a reversal of the process for these areas only. This is a difficult step to understand at first, but mastery of it will result in more attractive halftone work and will save countless hours of cutting.

4. Leave all the pure white areas — those which are to print as pure white in the final block print free of ink. If a portion of the photograph which will not blend well if printed in the solid color is to be removed, it may be left free of ink, in order to print white on the final block print. There are, therefore, two methods of eliminating unwanted portions of the photograph: By inking them in, in which case they will print in solid color; or by leaving them un-inked, in which case they will print as white.

5. Allow the ink to dry bone-hard, without blotting it. When the ink has dried, soak the photograph in cold water for five minutes, or until it is limp and flexible. Do not handle the surface. A slight amount of ink may 'bleed" off during this washing, but if a good quality of waterproof ink has been used, the main coating will stay intact.

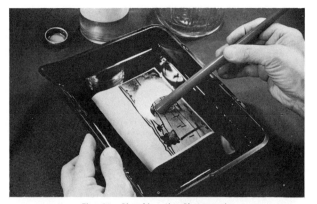
Fig. 94. Bleaching the Photograph

Fig. 95. The Bleached Photograph

6. Now, immerse the print in a bleaching solution. Use a flat tray and hold the print under the liquid until all the original photographic images have been bleached out, leaving only the inked drawing on the surface of the paper, Fig. 94. There seems to be no safe bleach which will reduce the darker portions to absolute white. However, for the purposes intended in this process, the formulas given below will reduce the photographic images to a very pale tan tone. Keep the print in the bleach for at least five minutes. The waterproof ink will not be affected by this bleaching process. Fig. 95 shows the photograph completely bleached out, leaving just the pen and ink drawing on the paper.

Prepare the bleaching solution by adding the following chemicals in the quantities indicated, to 16 ounces of water:

Fig. 96. Mixing Bleaching Solution in Glass Container
(Courtesy, Eastman Kodak Company)

Potassium ferricyanide .... 274 grains
Potassium bromide .... 274 grains
Potassium oxalate ...... 1 ounce, 283 grains
Acetic acid, 28% * .... 2½ drams

Perform the bleaching and mixing processes in enamel, glass, or hard plastic containers, Fig. 96. The quantities in the above formula are not absolute, and a little variation in proportion will do no harm. The formula will result in what is called a stock solution, which may be stored for several weeks in a tightly corked bottle. To use, mix one part solution with one part water to make the quantities desired. The bleach is poisonous if taken internally, and as with all chemicals, people with sensitive skin should handle it with caution.

If a bleach which does not contain acid is desired, the following formula, commonly called "Farmer's Reducer" may be purchased in a photographic supply store, or mixed by the craftsman:

Solution A

Potassium ferricyanide ....1¼ ounces
Water .... 16 ounces

* Acetic acid, 28% can be made by mixing approximately 3 ounces
of glacial acetic acid with 8 ounces of water.

Solution B

Hypo .... 4 ounces
Water .... 16 ounces

Mix one ounce of solution *A* with four ounces of solution *B* just before using. Proceed as with the previous formula. These solutions cannot be stored once they have been mixed. Follow the same precautions in mixing, handling, and using as with the previous formula.

7. After the print is completely bleached, wash it thoroughly in cold water until all the yellow stain caused by the potassium ferricyanide has disappeared. Then dry it between soft blotters under light pressure.

8. The dry print is now a pen and ink drawing of the original photograph, ready to be traced onto tracing paper and transferred with carbon paper to the surface of the linoleum. If the finished print is to remain in the original position from left to right, it will have to be transferred to the tracing paper from the inked drawing, through the *back* of the drawing, holding it on a sheet of glass over a lamp. When it is transferred to the linoleum, it will be in reverse.

Proceed with inking the drawing, cutting the linoleum, mounting on wood, and printing as outlined in Chapter V.

The craftsman will notice in the finished product the likeness to the original photograph, but he will also be aware of the limitations which all materials place upon the person working with them. It is never intended that linoleum block printing should be a substitute for the fine work possible on end-grain wooden blocks or copper and steel engravings. The linoleum block print, no matter how it is treated, looks, and should look, like a linoleum block print. It should be recognizable by its emphasis on large masses and areas instead of on detailing. Fig. 97 illustrates four different treatments of the same original subject using the various shading techniques shown in Fig. 92.

The advanced worker in linoleum block cutting may wish to experiment with the halftone and background techniques shown in Fig. 92. More involved photographs and even portraits can be converted into linoleum block prints.

Fig. 97. Four Different Shading Techniques
(Courtesy of the Hunt Pen Co.)

Fig. 98. A Photograph To Be Used for a Bookplate Design
(Courtesy of the Eastman Kodak Co.)

Additional Hints

1. When applying the ink to the photograph it is advisable to use a fine pen first, gradually increasing to larger and larger pens to fill in the larger areas. In this way, a better proportion between thicknesses of lines in the drawing will be maintained.

2. If an article such as a greeting card or a bookplate is being made from a photographic original, pen and ink lettering may be added to the surface of the photograph at the same time that the other inking is being accomplished. This lettering will then be part of the final pen and ink drawing, after the photograph has been bleached, Fig. 98. Since the entire drawing will be reversed for tracing, the lettering will be transferred to the linoleum in the reversed position.

CHAPTER X

Printing in More Than One Color

Printing in more than one color is known as *multicolor printing*. This technique enables the craftsman to broaden his area of operation almost without limit. Once the basic methods are mastered the linoleum block print can be made in as many colors or shades of color as desired. Fig. 99 shows a block print done in three colors. This simple flower design is appropriate for use on gift paper or other articles; the flower is red, the leaves are green, and the outline is in black.

Several principles are important in multicolor printing, and must be committed to memory before any attempt is made to work.

1. A separate linoleum block is made for each color to be printed.
2. The blocks must be cut so that the colors meet each other at the proper outlines.

Fig. 99. A Three-Color Block Print

Fig. 100. The Three Blocks Used in the Three-Color Print

3. An arrangement for printing must be so designed that each successive color is printed on the sheet in precisely the place desired.

4. Light colors should always be printed *first*, gradually running down the color chart through the intermediate colors, until the darkest color is printed *last*. If this is done, the slight overlapping of dark colors over light colors will not show.

5. The darkest color should form the over-all outline and should be designed to gather together all of the other colored sections on the print. Fig. 100 illustrates the three linoleum blocks required for printing the flower, as well as imprints of the three in separate colors. Fig. 101 shows the successive printing of each additional color.

In extremely advanced multicolor work points four and five above are not always followed. However, these techniques are recommended until considerable experience is gained.

The first step in multicolor work is to choose a design which will give large, solid areas. The flower design used in this chapter is such a design. The next step is the accomplishment of principles two and three above: Cutting the blocks accurately, and printing them so that the colors print where they are desired. This principle is known as *register*. The blocks are said to be cut *in register* and the printing therefrom is said to be *registered*.

Fig. 102 shows a device used for maintaining register in cutting as well as in printing. It is known as a register *jig*. It can be made in the home or school shop.

Procedure for Making Register Jig

1. The base board may be of any size or thickness. The one in the photograph is ½ inch thick and 10 x 14 inches in area. It has been found that this size will accommodate a print up to approximately 5 x 7 inches. The base board should be of flat, non-warped wood. Laminated plywood is recommended.

2. To this base board are attached two pieces of $\frac{1}{8}$-inch wood, one $4\frac{1}{2}$ x 14 inches and the other, $4\frac{1}{2}$ x $5\frac{1}{2}$ inches, forming an inverted "L". This arrangement leaves an open, angular area in the lower right-hand corner of the base board. This corner angle should be absolutely accurate. The $\frac{1}{8}$-inch wood is glued to the base board and then fastened with numerous flat-head screws, countersunk into the surface, to assure that the angle will not lose its shape.

3. The next piece consists of a strip of wood, the width of the base board (10 inches), placed on a perfect line with the edge of the upper strip of the inverted "L" ($\frac{1}{8}$-inch wood). This strip of wood, then, will be $4\frac{1}{2}$ x 10 inches and should be $\frac{3}{4}$-inch in thickness. It is hinged at the back so that it may be swung back when it is not used.

4. Sandpaper the entire jig thoroughly and finish it with a thin coating of shellac. While it is drying, cut several pieces of cardboard, approximately 5 x 7 inches, perfectly squared, to fit into the angular recess in the jig.

5. If the craftsman knows that he will always work with $\frac{1}{8}$-inch linoleum, the upper, hinged piece of wood may be omitted. By the same token, if the craftsman will always work with linoleum mounted on $\frac{3}{4}$-inch wooden blocks, this upper piece of wood may be fastened down, instead of being hinged. The pieces of cardboard are used to give slight additional height when working with various thicknesses of linoleum.

The next step is to trace the design on a large sheet of tracing paper. The colored areas are then filled in with crayons and the outline areas are inked to assure perfect outline edges. Remember to reverse the design if it is desired to have it print in the original position. All the materials and equipment are now in readiness for tracing the design onto the linoleum blocks.

Procedure for Making the Blocks
1. Cut three pieces of linoleum, exactly the same size, with perfectly square corners, Fig. 46.

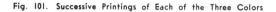

Fig. 101. Successive Printings of Each of the Three Colors

Fig. 102. A Register Jig

Fig. 103. Fitting the Linoleum in the Jig

2. On the back of each piece, on the burlap, mark an "L" with a pencil, in one of the corners.

3. Place one piece of linoleum in the recess of the jig, face up, with the corner marked "L" in the upper left. Make sure the linoleum fits snugly and tightly into the corner, Fig. 103. It is important that the

Fig. 104. Fitting the Design on the Jig

Fig. 105. Tracing Over the Design

Fig. 106. Placing the Cardboard Guides

surface of the linoleum reach *exactly* the same height as the height of the "L" shaped surface of the jig. Use the pieces of cardboard to adjust this height.

4. Attach the design tracing to the jig by using four thumb tacks, and in such a manner that the design is over the piece of linoleum, Fig. 104. If mounted linoleum

is used, lower the hinged portion of the jig and fasten the tracing to this instead.

5. Slip a sheet of carbon paper between the tracing and the linoleum, carbon side against the surface of the linoleum.

6. With a very sharp, hard pencil, carefully trace over the outlines of *one* color, Fig. 105.

7. Remove the linoleum and the carbon paper, being sure not to disturb the location of the tracing.

8. Place the second piece of linoleum into the jig, insert the carbon paper, and proceed to transfer the outlines of the second color area.

9. Remove the second block and proceed to transfer the final color (the outline) to the *third* block.

10. The tracing may now be removed and the jig placed aside until later.

11. All three blocks are then inked-in very carefully so as not to change the outlines in any way. Cut the blocks, leaving the areas to be printed standing high, and removing all of the balance of the block, Fig. 100.

When the linoleum blocks are completely cut and the ink removed, they are ready for printing in register.

Procedure in Printing

1. Determine the size of paper to be used and the location of the design.

2. Place a sheet of paper on the jig in the proper location so that the area to be printed falls over the recessed angle where the linoleum block was cut. Attach three or four small pieces of cardboard on the upper and left-hand margins of the paper, onto the jig, using rubber cement, Fig. 106. These will serve as guides for placing each successive sheet of paper in the same position on the jig.

3. Ink the block which was cut for the *lightest* color. Place it in the jig in the same position as when it was cut (with the corner marked "x" in the upper left), as shown in Fig. 107.

4. Place a sheet of paper on the jig, against the cardboard guides, being careful that

the sheet drops evenly onto the inked block, and does not smear, Fig. 108.

5. Print as many sheets in this first color as will be required for the completed project. You may wish to make a few extra copies, since some may be spoiled in printing the second and third colors.

6. The rolling pin method of printing (Chapter VI), the spoon method (Chapter VII), or even the copy press method described in the next chapter may be used for printing. The design of this particular jig makes it possible to insert it into the copy press as a complete unit.

NOTE: If mounted linoleum is used, the hinged portion of the jig is lowered into place as for the tracing operations, and the paper guides are attached to this surface. In all other instances this hinged portion is folded back, out of the way.

7. When the first color has dried on the sheets, the second block is inked with the *second* color to be used, and each sheet is then printed with the second color, in the same manner as the first color was printed. Care must be taken, however, that the block is fitted exactly into the angle (with the "*x*" in the upper left) and that each sheet is placed exactly against the paper guides.

8. When this second color has dried, the third and final color (the outline) is printed in the same manner as the first two colors were printed.

Procedure for Making a Baren

Some craftsmen prefer to use a *baren,* illustrated in use in Fig. 109, when printing multicolor blocks because it gives greater control of pressure, and there is less possibility of the paper slipping. The baren is merely a device with a hard, smooth surface, which can be rubbed across the paper to transfer the ink to it, Fig. 110. In this respect, the spoon, used for printing in Chapter VII, is a kind of baren. The ancient Japanese print makers used a baren covered with bamboo leaves to give it a smooth surface. Some modern craftsmen have substituted corn husks for the bamboo leaves. However, a piece of silk stocking as a covering will prove highly effective and easy to make.

Fig. 107. Placing the Block in the Jig

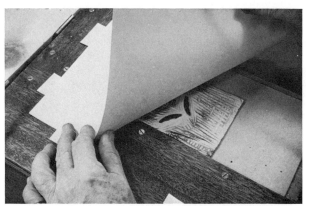
Fig. 108. Placing the Paper in Position for Printing

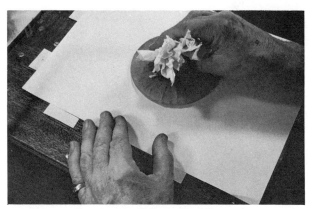
Fig. 109. Using a "Baren"

1. Cut two discs, about four inches in diameter, one of heavy cardboard and the other of corrugated box board.

2. Obtain an eight-inch square of fine, strong cloth (such as that taken from a discarded man's shirt), an eight-inch square of silk stocking, and a length of strong twine.

Fig. 110. A Baren

Fig. 111. Constructing a Baren

3. As in Fig. 111, place the piece of silk down first. On top of this place the square of cloth. Next the disc of cardboard, and finally the disc of corrugated board. Gather the cloth up, stretching it tightly around the discs of cardboard, and fasten

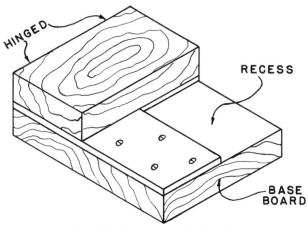

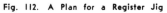

Fig. 112. A Plan for a Register Jig

it in place at the top by winding successive layers of twine around the gathering. Trim off some of the excess material thus gathered up.

4. The baren is used by rubbing the tight, silk surface back and forth across the back of the paper to be printed, as it rests on the inked block.

When the techniques of this chapter have been learned, the craftsman may wish to try multicolor block printing of as many as six or eight colors. However, the beginner is cautioned that the number of colors does not give the strength to a print. Rather, it is the manner in which color is used and the pleasing combinations decided upon.

Additional Hints

1. If difficulty is encountered with the tracing paper ripping where the thumb tacks have been inserted, small pieces of cellulose tape may be attached to the tracing at the points where the tacks will enter. It is extremely important that these tack holes do not become enlarged because this will destroy perfect register.

2. Because of the time involved in making multicolor prints, even more attention should be given to making clean impressions. A smeared impression of the third color, for example, destroys *all* of the work done up to that point. Therefore, care should be taken to wipe off any smeared portions of ink which may be on portions of the linoleum *other* than the design.

3. Multicolor prints should be hung for drying between application of successive colors. Do not stack them one over the other.

4. For the first experiment in multicolor, it is suggested that the block which will print the black outline, be cut so that the outline *slightly* overlaps the other color areas. This will tend to hide minor errors in register.

5. Fig. 112 is a working drawing from which the craftsman may construct the special register jig in the home or school shop.

CHAPTER XI

A Photographic Silhouette Block Print

A silhouette of the head of a person, as illustrated in Fig. 113, makes an interesting and highly personal corner cut on writing paper or on a greeting card. The silhouette is obtained by first taking a photograph and then using the design obtained from the finished print as the pattern. This method, however, is not related to the method of converting a photograph into a block print as explained in Chapter IX.

To take a photographic silhouette any type of camera may be used. The important thing to remember is that the light must come from *behind* the subect and *into* the lens. The subject interrupts the light and thus forms a solid shadow or silhouette. The subject must be photographed from a side view, commonly known as the *profile*. Inasmuch as there will be no light, dark, and medium areas in contrast with each other, but only a solid black area against a white background, any but a profile view normally would not be recognizable.

Fig. 113. A Photographic Silhouette Profile
(Courtesy of the Eastman Kodak Co.)

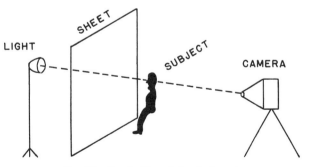

Fig. 114. The Position of the Equipment

Procedure

1. Arrange the camera, subject, and a photoflood lamp in a reflector, as shown in the drawing, Fig. 114. It will be noted that a sheet is hung between the lamp and the subject, so that a soft, diffused light strikes the camera lens. A doorway of a room is an excellent place to set-up for this photograph because the sheet can be hung in the doorway, with the lamp on one side of the sheet and the subject and the camera on the other side.

2. Set the lamp so that it is about two feet from the sheet. Place the subject as close to the other side of the sheet as possible without actually touching the sheet. The distance of the camera from the subject will have to be determined by the craftsman according to the kind of camera being used. Some cameras permit the attachment of a supplementary, close-up lens, which allows for the photographing of extremely close objects. Other cameras permit this close focusing with the normal camera lens, while still others restrict the photographer to approximately a six-foot distance from lens to subject.

3. Be sure the sheet has no wrinkles in it; these may show up in the photograph and destroy the even lighting required. Arrange the subject so that the full profile is apparent. The nose, chin, neck-line, etc., should be plainly visible.

4. Use the fastest film obtainable for your camera, and by using the manufacturer's instructions, compute the exposure necessary for the amount of light being used. The larger the lamp and the closer the camera is to the subject, the faster the exposure may be. However, it will be found

for most simple cameras that a slow exposure is necessary. Therefore the subject must sit still during the exposure time.

5. Adjust and focus the camera. Light the lamp, or have an assistant do this. Take the picture. When the picture is developed and printed it should appear as a rather black, solid, silhouette portrait against a milky white background.

6. Use this print as the design. Trace it onto tracing paper, and then proceed as before with transferring the design, cutting it, and printing it. Any color ink may be used for printing the linoleum block of the silhouette; however, black is usually associated with silhouettes.

Additional Hints

1. A photoflash bulb may be used in place of a photoflood, if it is of the type which may be screwed into an ordinary light receptacle. In this technique an assistant is needed. The photographer opens the shutter on *time* or *bulb*, signals the assistant to set off the flash bulb, and then closes the shutter.

2. Silhouettes may also be taken in natural sunlight by using the same technique of having the light come from behind the subject into the lens. However, since it is not usually practical in outdoor photography to use a sheet for diffusion, the sunlight, subject, and camera, set-up should be such that the direct rays of the sun do not strike the camera lens, but rather strike directly behind the subject.

3. Interesting greeting cards can be made from linoleum block prints by using the

Fig. 115. Putting the Linoleum Block in the Press

photographic silhouettes of families, children, or pets.

4. For variety and experience in technique it is suggested that the print of this linoleum block be made in the special linoleum block press shown in Fig. 39 or the copy press shown in Fig. 40, both of which are identical in construction and operation, except that one is of wood and the other is steel.

Place the sheet to be printed face up on a rectangle of cardboard of proper size to fit into the press. Ink the block and place it face down in position on the sheet. Over the linoleum, place a block of ¾-inch wood if the linoleum has not already been mounted on wood. Using the lower cardboard as a tray for handling, slide the entire stack into the press, Fig. 115. Lower the press to make the impression. Loosen the press, and again use the cardboard as a tray for removing the stack. Carefully peel the paper away from the block.

CHAPTER XII

Printing on Textiles

Printing on textiles is one height of accomplishment, producing articles of lasting value and great beauty, which can be laundered or dry-cleaned. Curtains, drapery material, slip-cover material, towels, table linens — these are but a few of the many articles which may be decorated by linoleum block printing. All the information covered in the book to this point will equip the craftsman to enter this extremely rewarding phase of block printing. Certain additional supplies and equipment will be needed. These can be easily obtained or made in the shop.

It will be assumed that the beginner has learned his lesson well, for in this application

Fig. 116. Inking the Design

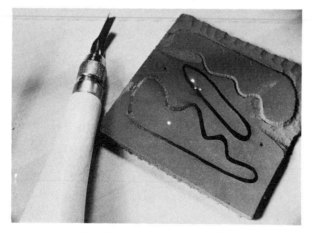

Fig. 117. Cutting Away the Linoleum

of the craft, careful attention must be given to *all* previous methods. For the sake of simplicity, certain limitations have been placed on its application. For more advanced techniques the worker should refer to the bibliography at the end of this book.

The methods of application have been limited to the following:

1. Applying the design on an open border such as found along the edge of towels and curtains.
2. Applying the design to form a closed border such as around the *entire* edge of a table cloth or kerchief.
3. Applying the design as an over-all repeat pattern.

   NOTE: The so-called "spot design" was introduced in Chapter V as a monogram.

The pigments used for printing must be bright, color-fast, and easily obtainable. These will be limited to the following:

1. Those which may be mixed at home or in school using printer's ink as a base.
2. Those which may be made from artist's oil colors with the addition of a special mordant (a substance which, when added to a pigment, makes the pigment permanent and insoluble).
3. Those which are obtainable commercially under the general heading of textile paints.

The basic steps in printing on textiles are the same as for preparing the block and printing on any other type of material. However, minor changes are required to assure perfect results. For that reason the basic steps will be reviewed at this point with the minor changes or special points of emphasis printed in italics:

Procedure for Making Block

1. The design chosen is drawn, traced, reversed, and transferred to the piece of linoleum as before.
2. The design is inked-in, Fig. 116.
3. The block is then cut with the linoleum cutter so that all unwanted portions are cut away. *The unwanted portions should*

be cut deeper for printing on textiles, because the print will be made on a soft, thick material rather than on a hard-surface paper and will therefore be pressed deeper into the impressions on the block, Fig. 117. It is assumed that at this point the craftsman is able to handle simple, solid area designs *without having to ink-in the entire area.*

4. Glue is applied to the block of wood and the linoleum is fastened to it. *For textile printing the linoleum must be attached to a wooden block. The block should be ¾-inch laminated plywood to insure a flat, unwarped surface, and must be cut perfectly square at all corners. The linoleum is mounted so that it is in perfect line with the edges of the wood, and small nails are driven through unused areas, into the wood, to insure absolute adhesion,* Fig. 118.

5. The block is inked in the usual manner, *except with the special textile inks and paints discussed later in this chapter.* Special care must be taken to wipe away any smears of ink which appear on surfaces other than those to be printed, Fig. 119.

6. *A movable or adjustable register device must be designed to allow the block* to be printed many times on the same article but *always precisely where it is desired,* Fig. 120.

7. *The mallet method* is used to do the print-

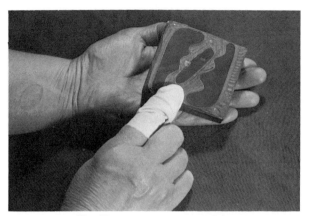

Fig. 119. Wiping Away Excess Ink

Fig. 120. Using a Register Device

Fig. 121. Using the Mallet Method

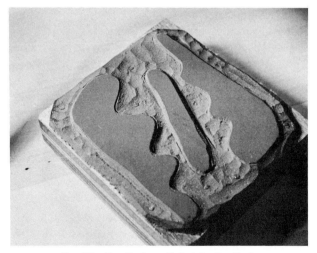

Fig. 118. The Linoleum Nailed to the Block

ing. The author has found no other method *completely* satisfactory. The foot method of printing, described at the end of this chapter may be used providing the work being printed can be stretched and registered on the floor rather than on a table. Fig. 121 shows the mallet being struck.

Fig. 122. Materials for Mixing a Mordant

The register device has been removed. *The block must be held perfectly in place and a sharp blow delivered to the block.* This is another reason for using plywood, as other types of wood may split from the force.

Textile Paint Made from Printer's Ink

Ordinary printer's ink in any color desired is mixed with a special mordant to make it insoluble and color-fast. One of the oldest known mordants is plain vinegar. It may be recalled that vinegar is added to many kinds of home dyes which are in use. Vinegar contains a greatly reduced and diluted form of acetic acid and is, therefore, too weak for this purpose. Full strength acetic acid is used in proper proportions with turpentine as a thinner for the ink, and with oil of wintergreen to add a pleasant odor to the substance, Fig. 122.

The following is a good working formula:

1 part of Acetic Acid
½ part of Oil of Wintergreen
12 parts of Turpentine

NOTE: In any basic formula, the term "parts" may be translated into any working unit desired. Thus, if the "part" were taken to mean one ounce, the formula would contain one ounce of Acetic Acid, one-half ounce of Wintergreen, and twelve ounces of turpentine. These quantities, incidentally, will make a sufficient quantity of this mordant to have on hand for a considerable amount of time.

Mix the three substances together and store the mixture in a tightly stoppered bottle, clearly marked, "Printer's Ink Mordant —

POISON." To use the mordant, add enough of it to a lump of printer's ink about the size of a marble to give it the thickness of syrup or heavy cream. Mix it on the plate glass with a spatula. It is then rolled out with the brayer so that a thin film is obtained and applied to the block in the usual manner.

Textile Paint Made from Artist's Oil Colors

This method is basically the same as the previous one with the following exceptions:

1. Artist's tube oils are used instead of printer's ink.

2. A commercially manufactured mordant is used instead of the mixture of acetic acid.

This method has several advantages: It does not require the purchasing of printer's ink if such is not available. The mordant is not poisonous, nor is it unpleasant to smell. This mordant is available under various brand names, such as, *Mixo* (The F. Weber Company), *Textine* (M. Grumbacher, Inc.), and others.

To use the mordant, squeeze a quantity of oil color from the tube onto a blotter. Allow to remain on the blotter for about fifteen minutes to remove most of the linseed oil used in preparing oil colors. Then mix it with the mordant on a glass plate, as before, until it is the consistency of heavy cream.

Commercially Made Textile Paints

There are almost as many textile paints on the market to bewilder the beginner as there are shades of colors. However, most of these are for various means of textile decorating other than block printing. To this author's best knowledge and belief, *Prang Textile Paint* (The American Crayon Co.) is the only commercial product generally available which is especially designed for block printing. The paints themselves are basic, in that they may be used for *any* type of application to fabrics. For block printing, a special substance is added to the paint (known as an extendor). The following formula is used for mixing the paint for block printing, Fig. 123:

2 parts of color paint desired
1 part of regular extendor
2 parts of hand blocking extendor

In the case of this particular product the *regular extendor* is actually the mordant, and the *hand blocking extendor* adds a quality to the paint which none of the other materials mentioned thus far, succeeds in doing: (1) It makes the paint more viscous (gluey or sticky) so that it may be applied more evenly on the block; and (2) It retards the drying speed so that the craftsman can work more slowly and carefully without fear of the paint drying on the block before he prints it.

To use this paint, mix the three components of the formula thoroughly on a glass plate with the spatula. Roll out a small glob of the mixture until a thin film is obtained and proceed as before.

In the use of any of the paints described above, the printed article must be thoroughly air-dried for at least twenty-four hours and then heat set with a hot iron (about 360° F.) The article is ironed on the printed surface with a damp press-cloth covering the painted portion, and then ironed on the reverse side for a total of three minutes under the heat, Fig. 124. The heat will complete the permanency of the print with the steam from the damp cloth aiding in penetrating the fabric. A steam iron may be used, but a press cloth should still be placed over the painted area because during this setting small particles of paint (not retained by the fabric and not needed) sometimes flake off.

If *Prang Textile Paint* is used, forty-eight or even seventy-two hours may be required for air drying (until dry to touch). Since this paint actually sets by heat the colors will appear brighter and with a better finish after they are heat-set.

All articles should be washed in mild soap and warm water after heat-setting to assure that the colors have "taken" properly (particularly if the article is to be a gift), and also to remove any finger smudges or other soiling marks. Ordinary ironing at temperatures recommended for the particular kind of fabric should follow drying.

It is suggested that the beginner try all three types of paints in an attempt to find the one he likes best. Certain colors and certain effects are produced more readily with one than with another.

Several centuries ago before the machine printing of fabrics was developed, block print-

Fig. 123. The Ingredients of Block Printing Paint

Fig. 124. Ironing the Finished Print

Fig. 125. A Block Printed Fabric of the 18th Century
(Courtesy of the Scalamandre Museum of Textiles)

ing of textiles had reached the level of a highly decorative, and extremely skilled craft. Fig. 125 shows a block print, printed in many colors, made in the late 1700's. However, the hand block printer of today working with linoleum must limit his design to keep within the range of his material. Bold, solid designs, monograms, geometric patterns, peasant motifs, name bor-

Fig. 126. A Name Design for Printing on Towel Borders

Fig. 127. A Draftsman's T-Square (Courtesy of M. Grumbacher)

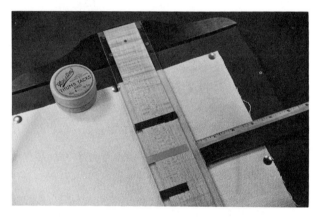

Fig. 128. Tacking the Towel to a Board

Fig. 129. Marking the Place for the Design

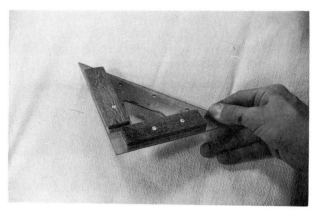

Fig. 130. A Draftsman's Triangle To Be Used as Part of a Register Jig

ders, and the like are examples of the types of designs which especially lend themselves to block printing.

Procedure for Open Border Design

1. Design an attractive arrangement of the first names of two people, which can be made into a block for printing on the edge of guest towels. Fig. 126 shows such a design.
2. Proceed with the tracing, reversing, and transferring of the design to the linoleum. Be sure to remember to transfer the design in reverse, so that it prints in the original position.
3. Cut the block, gouging the unwanted areas as deeply as possible to avoid their picking up paint later. Warming the linoleum, as explained in Chapter IV, will simplify cutting curves and some of the finer areas.
4. Obtain a length of huck toweling, approximately 28 inches long (the usual commercial width of huck is 18 inches). Using a draftsman's T-square (Fig. 127), square off one end by drawing a pencil line on the towel and then trimming it with scissors.
5. Tack the towel to a board that has been covered with several thicknesses of newspaper and a cloth outer covering, so that the cut edge of the towel runs parallel to the edge of the T-square, Fig. 128.
6. Allowing about one inch of material from the cut edge for hemming, determine how far from the hem the border design is wanted and place a small pencil mark at this point, Fig. 129.

7. The adjustable register jig for use in a border type print such as this consists merely of the T-square and a plastic or celluloid draftsman's triangle to which has been attached several blocks of wood to add height, Fig. 130.

8. Place the T-square on the towel so that it runs across at the point marked with pencil in step 6. For an open border design such as made for this project, it is customary to run the design from edge to edge, regardless of whether or not part of a design is cut off. Continuing the border as far as it will go lends charm to the finished product.

9. Set the triangle against the T-square, forming an angular corner into which the block can be fitted for printing as shown by "*x*" in Fig. 131.

10. Ink the block in the usual manner. Wipe off any excess paint which may be smeared on portions other than the design.

11. Carefully place the block face down in the proper position for viewing the design after it is printed. This can be simplified by printing the word "top" in bold letters on the back of the block, Fig. 132.

12. Strike the block one firm blow with a mallet.

13. Remove the block carefully. Slide the triangle over, keeping it against the edge of the T-square, to the next spot to be printed. Ink the block and duplicate the above procedure. Continue until the entire border has been printed, Fig. 133.

Fig. 131. Using a T-Square and a Triangle as a Registering Device

Fig. 132. Identifying the Top of the Block

Fig. 133. Repeating the Design

Fig. 134. A Closed Border Design

14. Hang to dry. Heat-set. Launder the article and it is ready for presentation.

Procedure for Closed Border

The second method of applying the design is that of the closed border as shown on the luncheon cloth in Fig. 134. This type of application requires careful computation with pencil, paper, and a ruler, to insure that the design will fit into the space available.

Fig. 135. A Suitable Design for a Closed Border Project (Courtesy of *The American Home Magazine*, Forest Hills, New York, where this pattern may be ordered)

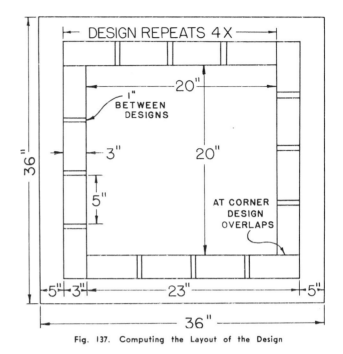

Fig. 137. Computing the Layout of the Design

Fig. 136. Measuring the Design

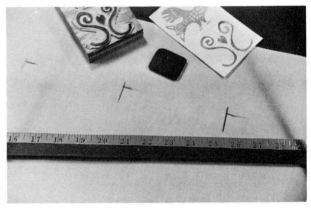

Fig. 138. Making Register Marks

1. Choose an appropriate design such as the one shown in Fig. 135.
2. Trace, reverse, transfer, and ink the design; cut and mount the block as in the previous method.
3. Make a print of the block on paper and measure the full dimensions of the design with a ruler, Fig. 136.
4. Prepare a scale drawing of a three-foot square, which is the size of the luncheon cloth in this case. The design layout is then computed as shown in Fig. 137. Note that the following measurements are considered in the drawing, the size of the design in this case being 3 x 5 inches:
   A. The distance of the border design from the edge of the cloth.
   B. The number of times that the design may be printed evenly spaced on each of the four sides.
   C. The amount of space to be left between each imprint in order to space the repeat designs evenly and to consume possible leftover space.
5. Register marks are now made on the cloth itself using a yardstick for a ruler and a

piece of tailor's chalk for marking. Make several angular marks on the cloth with the chalk wherever the block is to be set, Fig. 138. Use the chalk sparingly as it is difficult to remove. Either kerosene, benzene, or carbon tetrachloride will remove the marks later on, *after* heat setting but *before* laundering.

6. Proceed to print the entire closed border as explained previously.
7. The napkins to match this set carry a single design imprint. All pieces are hand frayed on the edges to maintain the character of a hand decorated project.

The following method of laying out a closed border for register may be easier for the beginner but requires additional preliminary work:

1. Print a large number of the designs on pieces of paper.
2. Using scissors trim each design perfectly square at the corners, cutting flush on a line with the design, Fig. 139.
3. Spread the cloth on a table and place the paper designs wherever it is desired to print them.
4. When these are completely placed, mark the location of each with tailor's chalk before removing the paper design.
5. Use these marks for registering the block while printing it.

Procedure for All-Over Repeat Pattern

The final method of applying the block print is in the form of an over-all repeat pattern such as used for drapery material, slip cover material, and yard goods in general. The de-

Fig. 139. Cutting Out a Design to Use for Layout Work

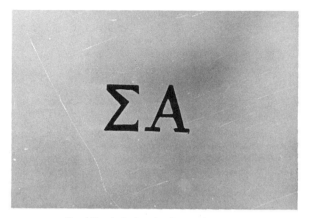

Fig. 140. A Design for Drapes in a Den

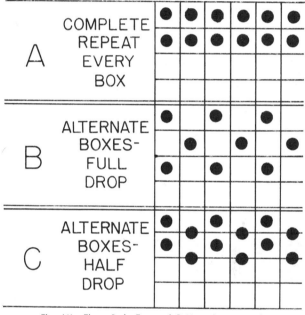

Fig. 141. Three Basic Types of Pattern Arrangement

sign chosen for this project, Fig. 140, is the emblem of an honor society, and is used for printing material to make curtains for a man's study or den.

1. Trace, reverse, transfer, and ink the design; cut and mount the block.
2. Decide upon the type of pattern arrangement wanted. Fig. 141 illustrates the three basic types of repeat arrangements used on fabrics. In *A* the design is repeated in each square, row after row; in *B* the design is printed in every other square, alternating on every other line giving the effect of a "full drop" of the pattern; and in *C* the design is dropped just half a

Fig. 142. A Large Triangle Made of Plywood

Fig. 145. Printing the Successive Rows of Design

Fig. 143. Marking the T-Square Where the Block will be Placed for Printing

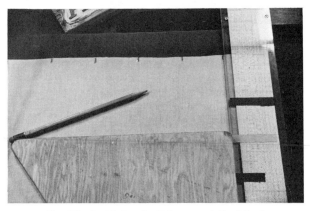

Fig. 144. Registering the T-Square and the Triangle

square. It must be realized that these squares are imaginary on the cloth and merely represent that portion of the cloth to be imprinted. All other repeat patterns are variations of these three basic repeats. In varying, the pattern may be rotated once each time it is repeated, or it may be inverted every other imprint, etc.

3. On the edge of the cloth to be printed make a small pencil mark indicating each line.

4. The T-square will once again be used, but in this project a larger triangle is often needed, therefore a special one is made from $\frac{1}{2}$-inch plywood, Fig. 142. However, one triangle, either this one or the smaller one used for the open border, may be made to serve both purposes.

5. Print the design on paper as in step 3 of the previous project. Measure the full dimensions as shown in Fig. 136.

6. On the edge of the T-square, using small strips of colored tape, mark each location where the triangle is to be placed for forming the angle which will receive the block for printing, Fig. 143.

7. For this project the layout of printing in alternate squares (shown at B in Fig. 141) was chosen. The alternate rows are marked as such on the edge of the T-square, using strips of tape of a different color, Fig. 143.

8. Spread the cloth out on the work board and tack it down on both edges. Place the T-square on the first pencil mark and place the triangle at the first point indicated by the strip of tape, Fig. 144.

9. Ink the block, wipe off surplus smears, place it in the proper spot at the angle formed by the T-square and triangle, and print it.

10. Remove the block. Slide the triangle up to the next register mark and repeat as in step 9. Continue in this manner across the entire width of cloth.

11. Slide the T-square down to the next pencil mark on the edge of the cloth, and continue as in steps 9. and 10., remembering to use the second set of tape register marks for each alternate row. Continue until the cloth is completely printed, Fig. 145.

12. Allow to air dry completely and then heat set. Wash, dry, iron, and it is ready for use.

One step has been omitted in the foregoing procedure in order not to confuse the beginner at the start; that is the preparation of the raw cloth before applying textile paint. Most fabrics are filled with a *sizing,* usually of starch or paste, which fills in the weave and makes possible the high finish found on new fabrics. Before applying textile paints this sizing should be thoroughly washed out with hot water and soap suds. The material will then have to be dried and ironed flat. Knitted materials do not contain sizings, nor do woolen materials. Linens sometimes do and cottons always do.

Before each textile printing job is undertaken, it is well to review the following points in order to insure that no difficulty will be encountered.

1. Remove sizing from cloth if necessary.

2. Lay out design on paper.

3. Set up the registering device to be used.

4. Make register marks as necessary on cloth and register jig.

5. Ink block, removing unwanted ink smears.

6. Complete all printing.

7. Air dry.

8. Heat-set.

9. Wash, dry, and iron.

Additional Hints

1. To determine proper heat of the iron used for the heat-setting operation, the following scale may be helpful:

Rayon	240°
Silk	300°
Wool	360°
Cotton	420°
Linen	480°

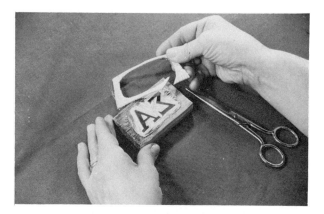

Fig. 146. Trimming the Linoleum

Fig. 147. Printing by Foot Pressure

These recommended temperatures are in Fahrenheit. Some irons have a scale on them which indicates the fabric type, while others indicate the temperature. The iron used for heat setting the paint should be approximately 360° or the temperature required for wool. This application of heat is continued for three full minutes. If the heat setting is being done on silk or rayon, the temperature will have to be lower and applied for a longer time.

2. To assist in eliminating smudges of ink on portions of the linoleum other than the design area when printing on textiles it is suggested that the linoleum be trimmed with scissors as close to the design as possible before mounting on wood, Fig. 146.

3. Foot pressure, Fig. 147, may be used to block a print when the register is maintained by marks made on the cloth, as in the closed border. It is not a practical method when a register device is used. The

block is placed in position, the foot is placed over it, and the weight of the body makes the imprint. This method may also be used for printing any of the blocks described in this book whenever the block is printed by placing it face down over the article.

4. Any fabric to be printed should be perfectly smooth and, preferably, stretched tight over the printing board. Wrinkles and folds should always be ironed out to prevent incorrect printing.

5. It must be emphasized that textile paints are designed to be permanent and color fast. This is even true to a great extent *before* they are heat set. Therefore, extreme care must be taken that no spot or dab of color is permitted to touch the cloth. Hands and equipment must be kept clean.

6. Occasionally, when nearing the completion of a large repeat pattern, due to the pressure of successive blows on the block and a faulty cutting of the linoleum in the first place, a small piece of the design may break away from the linoleum. With great care this may be glued back on using one of the commercial, waterproof, fast-drying cements. Or, if it is a large, solid area, the missing portion may be filled with plastic wood, and then sanded to the same height as the original design. Both of these methods, however, are makeshifts and will not substitute for careful planning and workmanship.

7. The author has found that hand-blocked cloths in over-all repeat patterns make excellent bookbinding cloth. After the cloth has been heat set and washed it is soaked for ten to fifteen minutes in a very strong solution of laundry starch. The cloth is then ironed while damp. Actually this replaces the sizing which should have been removed from the cloth at the start of the process to permit the paint to penetrate. When completely dried from ironing, the cloth is given a thin coating of varnish *on one side only* and then dried again. This varnished side is the outer side with the printed design on it. Tightly woven materials, such as linen and cotton, are best suited for this work.

CHAPTER XIII

Color, Color Mixing, and Types of Pigments

Volumes have been written about color and color mixing. Many theories have been published to simplify the area of color identification. Yet there still exists a great deal of mystery and confusion. The beginner is faced with series after series of puzzling identifications and the consumer is asked to choose from such a variety as wine red, burgundy red, shocking pink, citron, orange ice, luggage tan, peach, apple green, and heather, to name but a few. Despite this, any artist who works at his profession will tell you that he can paint almost any color he desires from a half dozen tubes of oil paint.

The important thing for the craftsman to keep in mind in all explorations into the study of color is that there are *three* primary (or basic) colors. Where these are obtained, how they are made, or why they are the color they are, are studies for advanced research workers. These colors are red, yellow, and blue. By mixing *equal* parts of any *two* of these colors, the *secondary* colors are produced. Thus, by mixing equal parts of red and yellow, *orange* is produced. *Equal* parts of yellow and blue produce *green*. *Equal* parts of red and blue produce *violet*. It is assumed that the worker in linoleum blocks will be able to name these basic colors of the rainbow despite the shade or depth they may be or what identification a manufacturer places upon the color. For this first step in the study of color the beginner is asked to call a *red* a *red* and an *orange* an *orange*, regardless of whether it is lighter or darker than others which can be found. This holds true for all of the *primary* and *secondary* colors: red, orange, yellow, green, blue, and violet. Fig. 148 represents these colors in chart form. To use the chart, run the finger across the top line until the first color being mixed is reached. Then run the finger down this column until it is opposite the color on the left representing the second color being mixed. The box in which the finger rests will be the color resulting when equal parts of each have been mixed.

COLOR MIXING CHART

	RED	ORANGE	YELLOW	GREEN	BLUE	VIOLET	BLACK	WHITE
RED	RED		ORANGE		VIOLET		MAROON	PINK
ORANGE		ORANGE		BROWN				
YELLOW	ORANGE		YELLOW		GREEN		OLIVE DRAB	PALE YELLOW
GREEN		BROWN		GREEN				
BLUE	VIOLET		GREEN		BLUE		NAVY BLUE	PALE BLUE
VIOLET						VIOLET		
BLACK	MAROON		OLIVE DRAB		NAVY BLUE		BLACK	GREY
WHITE	PINK		PALE YELLOW		PALE BLUE		GREY	WHITE

Fig. 148. A Color Chart

A *tint* of a color is produced by adding pure white to any one of the six colors mentioned. Thus, white added to red will produce *pink*, a color which all will recognize. An artist will tell you that the value has been increased by the addition of the white. In other words, more light is reflected back to the eye, thus creating an appearance of brightness. A *shade* of a color is produced by adding absolute black to any one of the colors. Thus, black added to blue will result in what most should be able to recognize as *navy blue*. Here again, an artist will explain that the value has been decreased by the addition of black; less light is reflected from the color back to the eye and the color gives the impression of having a darker appearance.

The chart in Fig. 148 also includes white and black. However, in these columns a number of colors are given names which may be disputed. It has been assumed that the few names given to these colors are generally recognized. All other combinations have been omitted.

The *tertiary* (or third order) colors are produced by mixing equal parts of any two secondary colors. It will be seen that this is the same as mixing unequal parts of any two primary colors. Thus, if green and orange are mixed in equal parts the resulting color will be brown. Since green contains equal parts of blue and yellow, and orange contains equal parts of red and yellow, then brown actually contains unequal parts of primary colors red, yellow, and blue. Only brown has been included in the chart because all other combinations produce colors which each craftsman had best identify for himself. It is in this area of color identification that the most confusion exists. It is suggested that the beginner place a glass plate over a sheet of white paper, and working in bright daylight, spread out a dab of each of the primary colors on one edge of the plate. By using a clean splint of wood or a match stick for each mixing operation, the secondary colors are mixed by taking equal parts of each of any two primary colors. Then, the tertiary colors may be mixed by taking equal parts of any two secondary colors. When this has been done, each color should have white added to part of the dab, and black added to the remainder of the dab. The result will be a visual display, before the individual's eye, of almost any color he will ever want to mix.

One further suggestion: Any time unequal proportions of colors are mixed, or more or less black or white are added to a color, completely different ranges of colors, including tints and shades are produced.

Imitation gold decorations can be produced in block printing by adding a goodly quantity of very fine grain, pale, lining bronzing powder to a light yellow block printing ink. Imitation silver can also be made by adding aluminum powder to a very light grey (black and white) block printing ink. In all such decoration, however, the bronzing powders have a tendency

Fig. 149. Ink Materials for Block Printing

to flake off with wear, so they should be restricted to use on such items as greeting cards or other paper articles which will be disposed of without too much handling.

Two other qualities of paints which the craftsman should become familiar with are *transparency* and *opacity*. A color is said to be transparent when the surface to which it is applied shows through it. It is said to be opaque when it completely covers the area and the surface cannot be seen. In general, all water color block printing inks are opaque. Oil-base block printing inks and printer's inks, are usually available in both types, opaque and transparent. In the specially-made textile colors it will be found that some colors are opaque and others tend to be transparent. However, when using oil-base inks or paints, other than those made especially for textiles, the classification of opaque or transparent will persist whether these are used on paper or textiles.

When using a water-soluble ink or paint water is the solvent or the material used to make it thinner in consistency. When using artist oil colors or oil-base block printing colors a small amount of turpentine may be used as the solvent or thinner. When printer's inks are used a very little turpentine or reducing varnish may be used as the solvent. In mixing the specially prepared textile paints and inks which are available commercially, the solvent should always be the one specified by the manufacturer.

Fig. 149 shows an array of paints, inks, pigments, and preparations which can be used in block printing on cloth or paper or other articles. Some of these items are standard products such as printer's inks and oil colors. Some are especially manufactured for block printing. Others are solvents which, when added to oil colors, make them washproof, color fast, etc. An art supply house will be able to answer many questions concerning materials. Some special methods of mixing standard paints for use on textiles to resist laundering and dry-cleaning are explained in Chapter XII.

CHAPTER XIV

Using a Printing Press for Linoleum Block Printing

A more advanced method, but not one beyond reach of the average school printing shop, is that of printing the linoleum block in the letterpress, Fig. 150. This method has the advantage of printing an unlimited number of copies, accurately registered, and much more quickly than any of the hand methods.

It is not the intention of this chapter to give a basic course in letterpress printing, but rather to assume that a knowledge of this will be required before undertaking this method.* Excellent results may be obtained by using any of the other methods described in this book, but those interested should be aware of the fact that the letterpress can be used for such work.

The most important item that must be learned when printing the block in a letterpress is that the linoleum *must* be mounted on wood, and the total height (from the back surface of the wooden block to the printing surface of the linoleum) must be .918 of an inch (or, approximately 11/12 of an inch). This height is known as "type high" and refers to the height of a piece of standard type from the foot of the type to the printing surface. All printing presses are manufactured to accommodate this height. The height may be determined by using calipers or a machinist's rule. The best method, however, is by using the type high gauge shown in Fig. 151. The linoleum block cut, mounted on wood, is slipped in between the machined faces of this gauge. If it is too high it will not fit. If too low it will slide through loosely. It should fit just right to the touch. A convenient method of arriving at the proper height is to mount $\frac{1}{8}$-inch linoleum on $\frac{3}{4}$-inch plywood. This results in a total height of .875 of an inch. The balance may be made up by pasting layers of thin paper to the back of the block. The block should be perfectly flat, smooth, and free of warp. For this reason plywood is recommended. The method of mount-

Fig. 150. A Letter Press (Courtesy of American Type Founders)

Fig. 151. The Type High Gauge (Courtesy of the Challenge Machinery Co.)

---

* *General Printing*, Cleeton, Glen U., and Pitkin, Charles W. McKnight & McKnight Publishing Company, Bloomington, Illinois, gives basic information in letterpress work.

Fig. 152. Locking the Linoleum Block into the Chase

Fig. 153. The Quoins (Courtesy of the Challenge Machinery Co.)

Fig. 154. The Quoin Key (Courtesy of the Challenge Machinery Co.)

Fig. 155. The Chase Placed in the Bed of the Press

ing linoleum on wooden blocks is explained in Chapter IV.

When the block is mounted and is of correct height it is then locked in the chase, Fig. 152. When tightening the quoins (the wedge-shaped pieces of metal used for holding the lock up in the chase), shown in Fig. 153, with the quoin key, Fig. 154, care should be taken not to exert too much pressure. If the wooden block has been cut by hand it may possibly be off-square by as much as .015 of an inch. Since the chase is made for perfectly shaped locking-up, the exertion of too much pressure may snap it; it is better to make an error in the direction of too light a pressure with the quoins, rather than too strong a pressure.

The chase is then placed in the bed of the press, Fig. 155. The remaining steps in the process, known in the trade as makeready are the same as for any work being printed in the letterpress. These are: making an impression on the tympan, placing the guide pins which will guide each piece that is printed, cleaning the tympan, and feeding the press. The details of these operations shall not be explained in full in this book. One step, however, must be mentioned in more detail.

Due to imperfections in the linoleum and possible warping of the block, neither of which is found very frequently when working with metal type, the impression may not strike evenly over the entire surface. In other chapters describing other methods of printing, this difficulty was corrected by various manual methods. Since the operator does not have control of the pressure in a letter press, and since this pressure is presumed to be even, the areas which do not print properly have to be corrected in another way. One method for correcting this is by using an *underlay*, which is a thin patch of paper (or several thicknesses, depending upon how much height has to be gained) pasted under the wooden block in the chase. The other method is by using an *overlay*. In this method small patches of the same thin paper are pasted on the tympan, and when the proper impression is made another tympan paper is placed over the one containing the overlays.

An interesting project which can be made in part by the linoleum block cut printed in the letterpress is the checkerboard shown in Fig. 156. Linoleum is cut into the number of black squares needed for one-half the checkerboard. These are mounted on a wooden block as described previously. The half-sheets are then printed in the press, with black ink on any color of construction paper. Two pieces of cardboard form the two halves of the checkerboard. Bookbinder's cloth or cloth from an old window shade are used for attaching the two cardboard pieces together to form a hinge. Colorful wall paper is attached to the outside panels of the checkerboard and the checkered sheets are attached to the inside. The same type of cloth is then used to put a binding around the entire checkerboard. Fig. 157 shows the linoleum squares mounted on wood.

Letterheads, greeting cards, and other items on which printing of some kind has been done over a background area of a light color on white paper are often seen. This color background is known as *tinting*. Tinting is accomplished in the same manner as the checkerboard squares were printed. A piece of linoleum is cut to the size required for the color background. It is mounted on a wooden block and the sheets are then printed in the tint of color desired. When this has dried on the paper, the balance of the lettering or other printing is impressed on top of the colored area.

It is sometimes desired to print a linoleum block cut and type at the same time. In the case of a letterhead such as that described in Chapter VIII it would be an advantage to have all of the printing done in one process if the block and the lettering were to be in the same color. This is accomplished by setting the type in the usual manner, Fig. 158. Then the linoleum block and the type are locked up at the same time. Proceed with the printing as before.

Fig. 156. A Project for the Letter Press

Fig. 157. The Linoleum Squares Used To Print a Checkerboard

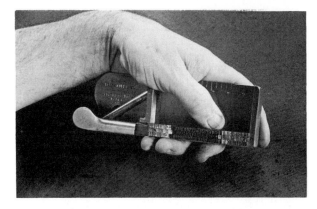

Fig. 158. Type for Printing a Letterhead

CHAPTER XV

Other Uses for Linoleum Blocks

This chapter describes a few additional applications of linoleum blocks, some of which do not rely entirely upon block printing. Also included are several suggested re-uses for the blocks after the printing is done as well as a decorative technique using the basic skills explained in Chapter II. Additional uses result in new ideas for gifts and for personal use, as

Fig. 161. Indicating the Divisions of the Design

Fig. 162. Going Over the Division Lines

Fig. 159. A Good Design for an Imitation Stained Glass Panel

Fig. 160. A Stained Glass Window (Courtesy of the Metropolitan Museum of Art)

well as in stimulating the mind of the creative craftsman in applying his skills to broader areas.

An Imitation Stained Glass Panel

For this project choose a picture or design which would look well when the entire view is accomplished in broad lines that divide the various areas into well-defined parts. Fig. 159 illustrates such a picture. In a stained glass panel lead strips divide each section of the glass, Fig. 160. The divisions, however, must be made in logical places. Outlines of the figure, natural folds in garments, natural lines in the body, or the outlines in a geometric design make logical divisions.

Trace the design so chosen and then with a pencil indicate with heavy lines on the tracing where these divisions are to be made, Fig. 161. With a very large drawing pen and black drawing ink go over all the lines, making each line the width which it will be in the final printing, Fig. 162. Transfer the design to the linoleum, ink it in, and cut the block as previously explained.

Using black printer's ink, print the block on a sheet of strong but somewhat transparent paper, such as tracing paper or typewriter second sheets. When the block print has dried, color the various sections as desired, using an artist's brush and oil paints. An experimental panel may first be made on which the colors are filled in with colored pencils or crayons.

After the oil colors have dried, coat the entire surface of the paper with a fast-drying, clear varnish, applying the strokes evenly and brushing the varnish from the center of the paper outward to the edges, Fig. 163. Hang in an upright position to dry so that the surplus varnish may drain off toward the lower edge.

When the varnish has dried, the "stained glass" will have a glossy finish and will resist wear from handling. It may be mounted on a lamp shade or it may be mounted between sheets of glass, the edges bound with cloth tape, and hung on a window as a centerpiece for other bric-a-brac, Fig. 164.

Resist Dyeing Using Block Prints

The art of resist dyeing is used commercially on fabrics in which it is desired to have the design itself show in the original fabric color, free from any other dye, while the entire background is colored with dye or paint. It is an ancient art and is closely related to tie dyeing in which portions of the fabric are tightly tied with thread before dipping the fabric into the dye. These are later opened and the tied areas have remained the basic fabric color.

There are many variations in methods of resist dyeing but common to them all is the technique of first printing the design with a substance which will *resist* the dye or paint and then removing the resist material after the dye or paint has dried. A good resist material for the beginner to use is a mixture of thin, prepared glue and white water paint, Fig. 165. The water paint is added mainly to enable the worker to see the mixture. The substance

Fig. 163. Varnishing the Design

Fig. 164. The Stained Glass Design as a Centerpiece

should be thick enough and tacky enough to adhere to the linoleum block.

It is recommended that white cloth be used for the first experiment as any color dye will prove effective when coloring white cloth. The glue mixture is applied to the linoleum block

Fig. 165. Materials for Making a Dye Resist Print

Fig. 166 A Linoleum Placque

Fig. 167. Linoleum Hot Plate Holder

with a brayer in the usual manner. For the printing the mallet method is suggested, Fig. 165. Allow the printing to dry completely. When dry, tack the cloth over thick layers of newspaper onto a board or an old table top. Since the resist in this case is water-soluble, the dye or paint which is used must be oil-soluble so as not to dissolve the resist. Use artist's

Fig. 168. Decorating a Tin Can

oil color, printer's ink, or one of the commercially available textile paints thinned to brushing consistency. Then with a wide paint brush (about one inch) paint over the entire cloth, covering designs and all.

When the paint has thoroughly dried (it may be removed from the board and hung to dry) heat-set the paint using a damp cloth and hot iron as explained in Chapter XII. Then wash the cloth in hot suds, scrubbing out the glue resist. The design imprint will now appear in white against whatever color was used to paint the fabric.

Making a Linoleum Plaque

After the linoleum block has served its purpose of printing, a coating of paint is allowed to dry on it. When this has dried, trim the edges perfectly straight, and apply a coat of clear varnish to the entire surface. The block may then be mounted on a panel of plywood and used as a wall decoration.

Making a Hot Plate Holder

If the linoleum block is large enough to permit a bowl or teapot to stand on it, it may be used for this purpose after the printing has been finished, Fig. 167. For this use, however, all paint should be scrubbed clean from the linoleum. Attach colored cloth tape around the edges. Do not varnish.

Block Printing on Painted Articles

Discarded tin cans, when properly opened with a rotary can-opener, cleaned of the label and glue, and painted white make excellent gift items for decoration, Fig. 168. Using the experimental technique outlined in Chapter II,

Fig. 169. An Art Gum Eraser (Courtesy of The Rosenthal Co.)

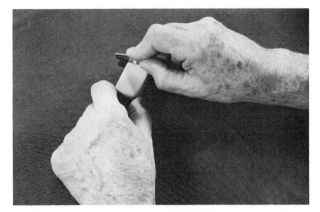

Fig. 170. Cutting the Eraser

take any firm-type eraser, Fig. 169, and cut through one end of it with a sharp single-edged razor blade to produce a flat, smooth surface, Fig. 170.

Carve the design out of this surface with a sharp pocket knife as shown in Fig. 9, page 15. After the tin can has been cleaned, prepare it by applying a smooth coating of white enamel to the outside, Fig. 171. Allow this to dry thoroughly and then rub it lightly with a piece of steel wool.

Using the eraser-cut design and a stamp pad as shown in Fig. 16, page 17, stamp the design in any arrangement desired on the white surface of the can. When the stamp pad ink has dried give the inside and outside of the can a coating of varnish. This same technique may be used for decorating trays, wooden boxes, kitchen cannisters, and discarded cans of all varieties. It is best to experiment first with the block on a piece of white card, as inverting the block alternately may create a more pleasant appearance.

Fig. 171. Painting the Can

With a little imagination attractive handmade gifts are completely within the reach of the beginner.

CHAPTER XVI

Alphabets

Almost any style of alphabet is adaptable to linoleum block cutting except the extremely ornate. However, it has been the intention of the author to stress that the craftsman should keep himself within the limitations of the medium in which he is working. It is held to be good artistic practice not to try to imitate another medium. If it is desired that the finished product look like a woodblock engraving or a steel etching, then the artist will ask, why not use wood or steel?

Linoleum block printing is particularly charming and attractive when bold, large,

broad areas are handled as complete white or complete colored sections. Fine line work, cross-hatching, and halftoning are reserved for special techniques. These same basic principles should be adhered to when facing the problem of alphabets. Fig. 172 illustrates a simple alphabet, emphasizing straight lines, which have the virtue of *looking as though it were cut from linoleum*. A solid, plain line letter, without bases, swirls, and other ornamentations, is the most satisfactory.

Many distinctive alphabets can be developed from this basic technique. Each craftsman is free to experiment with his own. Figs. 173 and 174 illustrate such alphabets and at the same time furnish the beginner with letters which may be traced.

The greeting card in Fig. 77, page 38, illustrates a solid, even line type of lettering which is both attractive and simple to cut. However, the designs based on letters illustrated in Chapter XII, are illustrative of the variety which is possible once the cutting techniques are mastered.

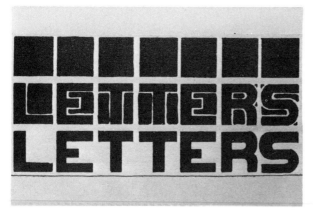

Fig. 172. Linoleum Block Lettering (Courtesy of the C. Howard Hunt Pen Co.)

Fig. 173. A Distinctive Alphabet for Linoleum Block Printing

Fig. 174. Another Good Alphabet Design for Linoleum Block Printing

The Care and Cleaning of Equipment

Most care and cleaning instructions have been given at appropriate places throughout the book. However there are always additional items of information which the craftsman should know. Good sound judgment is the best guide to the care and cleaning of any tools and equipment. A tool, no matter how inexpensive, should be treated in such a manner that it will always be ready for use next time. This is particularly true of cutting tools. The time to sharpen them is immediately *after* they are used and before they are stored away.

Cleanliness in handcrafts brings its own rewards. A sloppy craftsman will not produce acceptable work and soon will not be tolerated even by himself. In block printing, inks, paints, and dyes are used which are intended to be *permanent* once they are printed. There is no removing or correcting errors. Since the beginning of time man has stamped his mark and design on the things he used. If the mark was beautiful and well-done, history marvelled at it. If it was not well-done, history still viewed it. The bad as well as the good has a way of remaining for future generations to examine. Each craftsman should develop the pride in his work which will in turn develop neatness, orderliness, and cleanliness.

Care of Cutting Tools

These should be sharpened and honed on the stones shown in Fig. 22, page 21, until they have a razor-keen edge. The cutting edges should be protected from damage and from damaging the craftsman. They are best stored in a small box with no other equipment.

Special Cleaners

The most careful of craftsmen will at sometime require a special cleaning technique for removing stubborn paint and ink stains. Fig. 175 shows an array of cleaning materials, most of which have not been discussed in previous chapters.

Tincture of Green Soap

Since it contains alcohol, it is an excellent solvent for removing waterproof ink stains.

Fig. 175. Cleaning Materials

Gasoline

While not recommended for general use, it is not as disastrously dangerous to use as some would believe. Cleaning with it should *always* be done out-of-doors. It will usually remove dried printer's ink and dried commercial textile paint.

Benzene

A highly inflammable fluid, used actually as fuel for pocket lighters. It accomplishes a quicker and less oily job of cleaning than kerosene does. It should also be used out-of-doors or in a garage.

Carbon Tetrachloride

This is the finest non-inflammable, non-explosive, solvent obtainable at a reasonable cost. It actually puts fires out and is used in fire extinguishers. It is obtainable under the chemical name or under several famous brand names. It is particularly good for removing textile paints from the blocks. Its fumes should not be inhaled.

Steel Wool Pads

These are obtainable with a fine commercial soap solidified into the steel wool. They are excellent for scrubbing off the glass plate, the spatula, and even off the rubber brayer. They may be used to scour the surface of linoleum, if the surface is too oily to take the drawing ink.

Hand Brush

This is excellent for use in conjunction with any type of cleaner or solvent; it will reach deep impressions in linoleum blocks. Do not use a metal bristle brush such as used for finishing reversed calfskin leathers.

Rags and Kerosene

Plenty of both should be kept close at hand. It is better to soil a piece of waste rag than to soil a fine kerchief or tie which is being decorated. Kerosene is cheap, non-explosive, and quite a good solvent. Whenever oil-base paints are used, the block should be thoroughly cleaned with kerosene after use. This treatment will also serve to preserve the flexibility of the linoleum, since kerosene is slightly oily to the touch and does not penetrate in its cleaning properties quite as deeply as do some of the solvents.

A special word should be said about water. It should be used freely on the craftsman's hands both before and after he has been working. Where water-soluble inks are used, water may be safely applied to all equipment, including the entire block. This last may be immersed in water and scrubbed with soap.

A Calendar of Projects

September:
1. Kraft paper book jacket decorated with repeat patterns or school emblem.
2. A bookplate for school use or personal library use.
3. Greeting card for Rosh Hashana (Jewish New Year), which usually falls this month or in early October.

October:
1. Columbus Day design.
2. Hallowe'en napkins for parties.
3. Silhouette of pumpkin or witch printed on a "Trick or Treat" bag.
4. Special *Girl Scout Week design.*

November:
1. Book mark souvenir for *National Education Week (Open School Week).*
2. Program cover design for parent-teacher meetings.
3. Thanksgiving Day place cards or napkins.

December:
1. Christmas cards.
2. Gifts of block-printed guest towels.
3. Gifts of block-printed neckties.
4. Gifts of block-printed scarves.

January:
1. New Year's greeting cards.
2. Special design for *Boy Scout Week* (celebrated in February).

February:
1. Gifts for Valentine's Day.
2. George Washington or Abraham Lincoln patriotic motto card.
3. Special poster for celebration of *Brotherhood Week.*

March:
1. St. Patrick's Day decorated paper napkins for parties.
2. Block-printed gift paper to use throughout the year.

April:
1. Easter greeting card.

May:
1. Gifts for Mothers' Day.
2. Patriotic card for use at Memorial Day.

June:
1. Noteheads to use while on summer vacation.
2. Gifts for Fathers' Day.
3. Summer camp post cards with block-printed design.

July:
1. Patriotic motto card in red, white, and blue for Fourth of July.
2. Block-printed summer camp emblem on a T-shirt.

August:
1. Boy Scout Patrol emblem printed in black on red felt.
2. Block-printed stained glass panel to use as a gift.

NOTE: In planning any materials for use at specific dates, such as on religious holidays, legal holidays, and so on, it is necessary to begin preparations at least one month in advance. Certain religious holidays, as well as school-opening dates, vary from year to year. This information must be taken into account when making plans.

Bibliography

This book has described the earliest experimental stages in block printing, and the use of linoleum block prints for decorations on fabrics, paper, and other materials. It has given experiences with every popular printing technique, using almost every kind of ink and paint, applying the same to numerous useful articles. Each chapter may be developed to more advanced stages by the craftsman himself. However, for that craftsman who wants a little more or who has chosen this craft, now, as his very own, the following books are recommended. In general, those numerous books, which devote just a small portion of the text to a brief treatment of block printing, have been omitted from the list. Many of the very old texts have also been omitted since vocabulary and processes alike have changed so much over the years. The author is indebted to those who have gone before him and who have recorded their wisdom and findings.

Bone, Charlotte, *Linoleum Block Printing For Amateurs*. Boston, Mass.: The Beacon Press, 1936.

Corbin, T. J., *Hand Block Printing On Fabrics*. London: Isaac Pitman, 1934.

Dobson, Margaret, *Block Cutting & Print Making By Hand*. London: Isaac Pitman, 1932.

Hubbard, Hesketh, *Colour Block Print Making From Linoleum Blocks*. Salisbury, England: The Forest Press, 1927.

Perry, Raymond W., *Block Printing Craft*. Peoria, Illinois: Chas. Bennett Co., 1938.

Polk, Ralph W., *Essentials of Linoleum Block Printing*. Peoria, Illinois: Chas. Bennett Co., 1927.

Rice, William S., *Block Prints — How to Make Them*. Milwaukee: The Bruce Publishing Company, 1941.

Sprague, Curtiss, *How To Make Linoleum Blocks*. Pelham, New York: Bridgeman Publishers, 1928.

Watson, Ernest W., *Linoleum Block Printing*. Springfield, Mass.: Milton Bradley Co., 1929.

The following book is listed for its beauty and expert craftsmanship. It is illustrated in full page (8 x 10 inches) block prints, most of which are made from linoleum, and a few from wood:

Spelman, III John A., *At Home In the Hills*. Pine Mountain, Kentucky: Pine Mountain Print Shop. 1939.

Index